45 Business School (MBA) Recommendation Letters That Made a Difference

Dr. Nancy L. Nolan

3 1257 02388 1658

Copyright 2010.   Nancy L. Nolan, Ph.D.

Electronic, CD-ROM, and paperback versions published by:

Magnificent Milestones, Inc.
www.ivyleagueadmission.com

ISBN: 9781933819518

Disclaimers:

(1) This book was written as a guide; it does not claim to be the definitive word on the subject of recommendation letters.   The opinions expressed are the personal observations of the author based on her own experiences.   They are not intended to prejudice any party.   Accordingly, the author and publisher do not accept any liability or responsibility for any loss or damage that have been caused, or alleged to have been caused, through the use of information in this book.

(2) Admission to business school depends on several factors in addition to a candidate's reference letters (including GPA, GMAT scores, work experience and personal statement).   The author and publisher cannot guarantee that any applicant will be admitted to any specific school or program if (s)he follows the information in this book.

Dedication

For students everywhere;
may the size of your dreams be exceeded only
by your tenacity to attain them.

Acknowledgements

I am deeply indebted to the students, professors, employers, and admissions officers who have shared their perceptions and frustrations about recommendation letters. This book, which was written on your behalf, would not be nearly as powerful without your generous and insightful input.

I also want to thank my colleagues at www.ivyleagueadmission.com for providing a constant source of support, along with the best editorial help in the business.

45 Business School (MBA) Recommendation Letters That Made a Difference

45 Business School (MBA) Recommendation Letters That Made a Difference

Chapter 1: How Academic References / Recommendations are Used

For most candidates, few experiences are as daunting as applying for admission to business school. Competition is fierce at top US programs, where candidates search for every viable way to differentiate themselves. In an exceptional pool of applicants, even a slight difference in GPA and test scores can make the difference between admission and rejection. Ironically, in their zeal to make the best possible impression on the admissions committee, most candidates tend to overlook one of the most important aspects of the application: their reference letters.

Although academic achievements are important, they are only a small part of the admissions decision. Increasingly, top schools are placing greater weight on the quality and depth of your recommendations. As admissions officers, it is their responsibility to admit talented, multi-dimensional people with the potential to ascend to the executive level in their respective fields. To do so, they must evaluate not only your intellectual ability, but other traits that are not reflected by grades and test scores.

As a result, reference letters from credible third-party sources who can objectively evaluate your integrity and character are paramount in the evaluation process. In fact, they often play a key role in whether you are offered a seat in the class.

From our perspective, candidates don't place much emphasis on their letters of reference for two reasons:

1. they don't think they can control their contents
2. they don't know the specific steps they should take to improve their recommendations

This publication offers a viable plan for getting reference letters that convey *exactly* the attributes you want the admissions committee to see.

From our perspective, smart candidates give their reference letters that same level of attention that they give to their application essays. They take the time to find the *right* people to say the *right* things in the *right* level of detail. In a highly competitive applicant pool, the choice between two equally qualified candidates often comes down to the quality and depth of their recommendations. Choosing the wrong people to write your letters can have devastating consequences.

Sadly, most recommendations we see are short, vague and non-persuasive; they do little to convince us that the candidate is special enough to earn our support. Getting great letters requires planning, hard work and initiative, but is well worth the trouble.

What Makes a Great Letter?

A great letter supplements the data you have provided the school about your academic and professional history with independent corroboration of your performance and potential. It also provides critical information about your personality, ethics and integrity that isn't captured anywhere elsewhere in the application. The BEST references are short, specific and insightful. They are written by faculty members and seasoned professionals who know you well enough to share specific examples of your best traits.

Here is what the committee hopes to learn from your reference letters:

   a. Your specific qualifications, including the depth of your academic and professional experiences
   b. Your unique traits that aren't covered anywhere else in the application
   c. Your demonstrated commitment to pursuing a business career
   d. How you compare to other candidates with similar aspirations

From our experience, reference letters are the ONLY reliable indicator of several essential character traits, such as humor, maturity and tenacity. Many candidates write compelling essays to convince the committee that they are smart, funny team players, but it carries FAR more weight if an objective third-party confirms that. A thoughtful, well-written reference letter, which includes specific *examples* of a candidate's strengths, can make or break an application.

8

How Reference Letters are Used

As a general rule, recommendation letters supplement the primary admissions criteria for business school, which are your GPA and GMAT scores. In highly competitive programs, the applicant pool can quickly be sorted into three categories:

a. candidates with excellent grades and GMAT scores: good chance of admission
b. candidates who are borderline cases: application is competitive, but not outstanding
c. candidates with low grades and disappointing GMAT scores: poor chance of admission

Unfortunately, if you fall into category c, even great letters of recommendation may not save you from rejection. Highly competitive schools often screen out weaker applicants by imposing a minimum "cutoff" for GPA and GMAT scores. Although a reference letter can "explain" a disappointing score, it usually cannot compensate for it. Top schools will only give so much leeway to candidates who do not present a solid track record of success.

In contrast, reference letters for candidates in category a are usually disaster checks. These applicants have exceptional grades, top test scores and impressive personal statements. On paper, they are everything a business school is looking for. Their reference letters must:

a. validate their success
b. document their character, integrity and work ethic

For candidates in category a (excellent grades and test scores), a bad or mediocre recommendation can be extremely harmful. If your reference letters cast doubt upon the positive picture you have created (or reveal a serious character defect), the committee will be less likely to take a chance on you.

Surprisingly, nearly 70% of the applicant pool falls into category b, or borderline. These candidates have competitive grades and GMAT scores, but are otherwise not distinguishable from others with similar "numbers." Their acceptance or rejection often hinges on an exceptional intrinsic quality that captures the committees' interest and makes a positive impression. In some cases, this can be their commitment to family, their dedication to community service or their ability to overcome an obstacle. Reference letters from third parties who can document these activities can make or break their applications.

Chapter 2:   Who Should Write Your References

Before you ask anyone to write a letter for you, carefully review the instructions from each school where you plan to apply.   From our experience, each school takes a slightly different approach to the recommendation process.   Some accept free-style letters, while others expect the reviewer to complete a rating form that includes a dozen different attributes.   Some schools specify who should (and should not) write your letters, while others leave the choice up to you.

Schools also differ in the number of letters they require (and accept), with most requiring at least two (and accepting no more than five).   Follow each school's instructions *exactly*, regardless of how much it complicates the process on your end.   Remember, this is the school's first chance to evaluate how well you follow instructions; it's not the time to be a rebel.

As a general rule, schools expect to see reference letters from the following people:

1.   Your undergraduate committee or adviser
2.   A professor from your major field of study
3.   Your major professor, if you are a graduate student
4.   Your research advisor, if you have conducted academic research
5.   Your supervisor, if you are currently employed

In many cases, the school's requirements will automatically determine who writes your letters.   If so, approach each author with the information in this publication to ensure that you get the best recommendations possible.   On the other hand, if you have a choice of authors (or the luxury of submitting additional letters), try to pick the people who can best support your candidacy.

From an admissions perspective, a substantive letter of reference has three important features.   The author:

a.   understands the intellectual demands of business school
b.   knows you well enough to evaluate your qualifications
c.   is willing/able to provide enough supporting detail to justify his/her assessment

As a general rule, you should avoid sending letters from teaching assistants, friends, school alumni, relatives, clergymen or politicians, UNLESS they have personally supervised your academic or professional work and can comment on the specific attributes that are being evaluated in the admissions process. You'd be surprised how many people fall into this trap, not realizing that it actually hurts their chances. Nearly every year, business schools receive letters from Senators, Governors and famous Hollywood stars in support of candidates they barely know.   They are not impressed.   The admissions process is serious business, not a popularity contest.   The committee members are not so star struck that they will give a seat to someone just because her aunt works for the Governor.

Many candidates are surprised that letters from Teaching Assistants and Research Assistants carry little or no weight.   From an admissions perspective, TAs and RAs are simply not knowledgeable enough about the selection process to be reliable sources of information.   Business schools are looking for an honest appraisal of your character from people with extensive experience in the field. In academia, this is the tenured faculty.

Academic References

Surprisingly, even the best students sometimes have trouble producing exceptional letters of reference.   Getting great letters requires a considerable amount of planning, particularly in the following situations:

a.   At large universities, many classes are taught in large lecture halls that hold hundreds of students.   Even if you ace the class, the professor may not know you well enough on a personal level to make an honest assessment of your suitability for business school.

b.   Older applicants are at a disadvantage if an extended period of time has elapsed since they received their undergraduate degrees.   Even the best professors can forget individual students after an extended period of time.

If you are still an undergraduate student, here are a few tips to help you stand out in the crowd:

a. Get to know your professors
b. Sit in the front row and ask questions during class
c. Try to take an upper-division class with a professor you particularly enjoy
d. Arrange to do a research project with your favorite professor during your sophomore or junior year

If you have already graduated, keep in touch with your favorite undergraduate faculty members via email and holiday cards. Later, when you ask for a letter of reference, they will be up to speed on your post-collegiate accomplishments.

Choosing Your Authors

The best reference letters are from credible sources that can reinforce and complement the information on your resume. Your authors should:

a. be successful leaders, researchers or scholars
b. have worked closely with you in school or in a professional environment
c. regard you as a talented candidate with incredible potential
d. have sterling academic and professional reputations

Furthermore, these authors must be willing to state that they:

a. know you well enough to evaluate your suitability for an MBA program
b. have observed your growth and development over time
c. believe that you compare favorably to other candidates they have observed

From our experience, the strongest letters come from the following authors:

a. *Senior faculty members* with whom you have worked on a project. Try to get a letter from someone in your undergraduate major and another from a faculty member in a non-related field. You want to show the committee that you are a well-balanced person with strengths in diverse academic areas.

b. A *mentor* in your professional field, particularly if you have worked with this person for several years. Ideally, the author is a leader who can personally attest to your work style, personality and stamina.

c. A *supervisor from your participation in volunteer work or community service*. A well-crafted reference letter from an administrator of a non-profit organization who can personally attest to your devotion to an outside cause is highly perceived in the admissions process. The letter should cite the specific contributions you have made to the organization and your ability to get along with different types of people. These references, if chosen wisely, can make your application unique and memorable. They can also document how you have used your skills in an altruistic manner.

d. Your *boss or supervisor*, if you are currently working full-time. For older candidates, this is your chance to update the committee on what you have accomplished since you graduated from college. In most cases, there is a large difference in maturity between a 22-year-old recent graduate and a 27-year-old with several years of experience. Your reference letter from your employer should explain the type and extent of your professional experiences and how they have influenced your goals. Your supervisor can give the committee a first-hand account of your career progression, including the cultivation of previously unknown talents and skills.

Red Flags Regarding Your Choice of Reference Letter Writers

For what it's worth, here are the most common "red flags" regarding reference letters:

a. A candidate has excellent undergraduate grades, but does not submit a letter from a single faculty member. Many business schools will call the undergraduate institution to find out why.

b. A candidate has extensive professional experience, but does not offer a reference letter from his/her current employer. We understand that many candidates cannot risk their jobs by sending a letter from their immediate supervisor. In many firms, once your boss knows that you plan to resign to attend business school, your professional options will be limited. Business schools "get" that. If you cannot provide a letter from your boss without jeopardizing your job, you should submit a letter from a client or peer, rather than a supervisor. But you MUST send a letter from someone who can document your performance in your most recent position. If you don't, the committee will wonder what you are trying to hide.

c. A candidate who refuses to waive his right to see his reference letters. In the business world, reference letters are not cloaked in the same level of secrecy as in academia. In fact, most employers will give a candidate a copy of the recommendation as a matter of professional courtesy. If your authors extend this courtesy to you, that's terrific; you will know upfront what they have told the admissions committee about you. But don't insist upon seeing the letter if the author does not offer to show it to you. As a general rule, the admissions committee will view the letter as more forthcoming if you have waived your right to see it.

Challenges to Getting a Great Reference

Even the best candidates have trouble getting great letters. Here are the most common challenges, which we will address later in this publication:

1. Well-intentioned bosses and faculty members who don't know what to say. A great letter offers a critical analysis of your strengths and weaknesses from someone who knows you well enough to make an impartial assessment. The details must reinforce and complement the information in the rest of your application. In selecting your reference writers, you must make sure that they:

a.   are good writers
b.   know what to say
c.   support you without reservation

Be VERY selective in who you ask.

2. Authors whose native language is not English. The best references discuss subtle nuances of a candidate's personality and professional skills, which requires a strong proficiency in written English. Authors who are uncomfortable with the language tend to write less, which ultimately hurts the candidate.

3. Faculty references who don't understand the non-academic aspects of the selection process. Top-tier MBA programs attract candidates from disciplines as diverse as art history and geophysics. To gain admission to these programs, applicants must demonstrate skills that are not taught in their undergraduate course work. From our experience, many faculty references simply say, "Sam's academic record speaks for itself." Unfortunately, this is not helpful for highly competitive programs, where leadership and interpersonal skills are as highly valued as academic success.

4. Harried bosses and faculty members who don't have the time to write the letters for you. Rather than decline, they do a haphazard job, which does not enhance your candidacy.

5. Employers who refuse to offer any information beyond your title, salary and dates of employment. For legal reasons, many companies have taken a hands-off approach regarding recommendations; they either refuse all requests or limit their comments to names, dates and titles. Some firms even insist that all letters sent out on their corporate stationary be approved by a manager in human resources, who may not even know you. When you approach someone about writing a letter, don't automatically assume that (s)he has free reign to use his/her corporate logo however (s)he chooses. Company rules may severely restrict what current employees are allowed to say. Make sure that the person you have selected is free to write the type of detailed, enthusiastic endorsement that you need. If not, ask someone else.

6. Authors who instruct the candidate to write his/her OWN letter, which they agree to sign. This is a candidate's dream, until (s)he sits down to write. Sadly, most applicants lack the experience to assume the perspective and tone of someone in the recommender's position. They also don't really know what the committee expects. After viewing thousands of references, most admissions officers have an excellent feel for authenticity. As a result, letters written by the actual candidates are embarrassingly easy to spot (and they are the kiss of death for the applicant's admission chances).

Fortunately, there are ways to tackle each of these challenges and get the letters you deserve. Read on!

Chapter 3:   Using the Rating Scale as a Guide

In most cases, each business school will provide its own evaluation form for your reference writers to complete. Although all forms are somewhat different, the one shown on the next page (and in Appendix 1) is a fairly representative sample, which we will use for discussion purposes in this publication.   Before you ask *anyone* to write a letter on your behalf, take a look at the evaluation form that each school expects him/her to complete.   Study the list of attributes that the writer must assess.

On our sample form, the attributes easily consolidate into four distinct categories:

1.   **Academic Ability**:   intellectual curiosity, scholarship

2.   **Motivation**:   reliability, perseverance

3.   **Professional Strengths**:   judgment, resourcefulness, communication skills

4.   **Personal Strengths**:   interpersonal relations, emotional stability, self-confidence, empathy, maturity

Note that only a few categories involve your GPA or academic performance.   Even fewer relate to your mastery of any specific subject matter.   Instead, the attributes are *intrinsic character traits* that govern your behavior in all aspects of your life. The BEST letters will come from people who are willing and able to discuss these traits in detail.

Before you ask someone to write a reference letter, take a few moments to list the ways that you have exemplified the traits on the rating scale.   Restrict your observations to achievements and activities that your author *has actually observed*.   Next, for each trait that you have selected, provide a specific example.   These observations, which we will call your "**Match Points**," will form the foundation of your reference letter.

Sample List of **Match Points**   (for Dr. Martin's letter)

1.   **Scholarship**:   completed three of Dr. Martin's psychology classes with an A grade.   Completed my BA in Psychology with a perfect 4.0 GPA.

2.   **Communication skills**:   excellent speaker and writer;   my oral presentation at the 2004 Annual Meeting of the American Psychological Association won third place in the national competition.

3.   **Empathy**:   high emotional intelligence;   assumed workload for a fellow student after a debilitating car accident. Visited the student often during her medical leave and provided a consistent source of emotional support.

4.   **Language Skills**:   fluent in English, Spanish and Russian; frequently translate documents and journal articles for the head of the psychology department.

5.   **Motivation**:   assumed leadership responsibilities in the lab, including the supervision of two lab assistants.   With their support, I completed a side project that yielded two publications in the *Journal of Adolescent Psychology*.

We will discuss this list further in Chapter 4.

Sample Rating Sheet

Factors: For each factor below, please indicate your opinion of this applicant's rating on that factor relative to other candidates you have observed.

Ranking Standards:

1. Exceptional, top 5%
2. Excellent, next 10%
3. Good, next 20%

4. Average, middle 30%
5. Reservation, next 30%
6. Poor, low 5%

7. No basis for judgment

Factors:

_____   **Emotional Stability:**   Exhibits stable moods; performs under pressure

_____   **Interpersonal Relations:**   Rapport with others; cooperation, attitude toward supervisors

_____   **Judgment:**   Ability to analyze problems, common sense; decisiveness

_____   **Resourcefulness:**   Originality; initiative, management of resources and time

_____   **Reliability:**   Dependability; sense of responsibility, promptness; conscientiousness

_____   **Perseverance:**   Stamina; endurance, psychological strength

_____   **Communication skills:**   Clarity in writing and speech

_____   **Self-confidence:** Assuredness; awareness of strengths & weaknesses

_____   **Empathy:**   Consideration; tact; sensitivity to the needs of others

_____   **Maturity:**   Personal development; social awareness, ability to cope with life situations

_____   **Intellectual curiosity:**   Desire to learn and extend beyond expectations

_____   **Scholarship:** Ability to learn, quality of study habits, native intellectual ability

_____   **Motivation:**   Depth of commitment; intensity; sincerity of career choice

Evaluation Summary:

Compared to other business school applicants you know, please provide an overall evaluation of this candidate:

( ) Exceptional candidate, top 5%
( ) Excellent candidate, next 10%
( ) Good candidate, next 20%

( ) Average candidate, middle 30%
( ) Weak candidate, bottom 35%
( ) No basis for judgment

Universal Traits that Business Schools Seek

If at all possible, have your reference letters validate the following universal strengths, which are essential in a business career:

Exceptional language skills. Write and speak clearly and concisely. Responds to questions (and dissenting opinions) with confidence and grace. Excellent listing skills - can pick up subtle distinctions in discussions and debates.

Excellent analytical skills. Can think independently and make decisions that require the use of various types of reasoning. Can distinguish relevant details from extraneous information in a data set or case study. These skills are often honed in science, mathematics, logic, and economics classes, which require the integration of data from multiple – and often conflicting –sources.

Thinks "outside the box." In emergency situations, there are rarely hard-and-fast rules to guide a person's judgment. Successful candidates can tolerate this ambiguity and recognize the exceptions that modify general rules. Business schools need to know whether an applicant is likely to be stimulated (or frustrated) by questions (and scenarios) that have no "correct" answers.

Thrives in a rigorous, interactive environment. Candidates who enjoy rigorous discussions and collaborative projects are more likely to flourish in the competitive atmosphere of business school. Additionally, students must be diligent and well-organized to keep pace with the amount of reading and memorization that business school requires. A mature attitude and healthy sense of humor are highly prized in the selection process.

Chapter 4: How to Ask for a Reference Letter

Once you have chosen your potential reference writers, you need to ask them if they are willing to tackle the job. Don't assume that every person you select has the time, energy or inclination to write a great letter of recommendation. Thankfully, by following these tips, you can maximize your chances of getting the *right* people to go to bat for you.

a. **Approach.** Don't simply call or send a form to your writers; always arrange for a personal meeting, if possible, or make a phone call to discuss your request (if the writer is not geographically close). Explain your desire to attend business school and your need for a comprehensive letter of reference. Discuss any issues or concerns the person has about your candidacy.

Verify orally that (s)he is willing to write a "strong letter of support," not just an average or lukewarm one. If the person declines, do not push the issue. If you sense any hesitation, graciously withdraw the request. You are better off asking someone else who can recommend you without reservation.

A face-to-face meeting also gives the writer an opportunity to ask clarifying questions. For example, which letters are mailed directly to the school and which letters are returned to the student? Which envelopes must have the professor's signature on the seal? When is each letter due? By discussing these requirements with your writers in person, you can ensure that your letters arrive at the right place by the stipulated deadlines.

During your initial conversation, feel free to mention the attributes you would like the letter to highlight; make sure that the person concurs with your own self-assessment. Although it is awkward (and somewhat embarrassing) to discuss your perceived flaws, it is *far* better to identify a non-supportive author now, rather than obtain a bad letter of recommendation.

b. **Documentation.** If the person agrees to write an enthusiastic letter, give him/her the following information:

    i.   A cover letter with the names, addresses and deadlines for every letter you need   (Appendix 2)
    ii.   The appropriate forms from each school that (s)he will need to complete
    iii.   A summary of your "Match Points," which explain your fit for the program you have chosen   (Appendix 3)
    iv.   A current copy of your resume
    v.   Your personal statement
    vi.   Pre-addressed, stamped envelopes for all letters

These documents will make the writer's job easier because they provide the relevant details for him/her to include in the letter. They will also set you apart from the crowd. In my career, I've written hundreds of letters of recommendation for students who were seeking jobs, advanced degrees, scholarships and fellowships. Only a small handful have ever provided this information, which is crucial for writing an effective letter. I am always impressed when a candidate takes the time to organize his/her needs and focus my energy in the right direction. By doing this, (s)he already demonstrates many of the skills that are necessary for success.

Increasingly, MBA admissions committees expect writers to support the claims that they make in letters of recommendation. If a professor says "John is a persuasive speaker," (s)he must provide concrete evidence that John is actually a persuasive speaker. Unfortunately, few faculty members keep copies of student papers, quizzes or descriptions of a student's participation in the classroom. For this reason, you should customize the information on your Match Points for each individual author. Remind each person of your accomplishments in his/her class or department; include specific details. Don't assume that they have the documentation on hand to write a great letter.

A caveat for candidates who are still enrolled in their undergraduate studies; from my experience, many college seniors do not have a particularly well-organized resume. For academic references, make sure that your resume includes all of the information the author will need to draft a detailed letter. At the very least, please include:

a.   your overall GPA
b.   your major and minor
c.   the titles and abstracts of any research papers you have written
d.   honor societies to which you belong

e. awards you have won
f. activities in which you have participated (and any offices held)
g. work experience
h. service activities and volunteer work
i. a description of your professional goals

By providing this information in a clear and concise format, you can help your authors make their best possible case for you.

c. **Timing.** Arrange for your reference letters no later than September in your senior year of college (for candidates who have already graduated, at least *six weeks* before you submit your application).   Ideally, ask in the middle, rather than the end, of a semester. Usually, by semester's end, most professors are overwhelmed with requests for letters and yours will simply be another request in the pack.   To increase your odds of receiving a more thorough recommendation, submit your request before the big rush.

Tell your reference writers all of the places you are applying at your initial meeting, so they can prepare all of the letters at the same time. Don't blindside them with requests for additional letters later on.   From my experience, it's far easier to send out many letters at once than one or two at a time.

d. **Copy of the letter**. Without exception, you should waive the right to see all of your recommendations. Admissions committees place little stock in letters that the applicant insists upon seeing, because they know that the author is less forthcoming than if the reference was confidential.   You may, however, ask the author to send a *copy* of the letter to you for your files.   This is not a violation of the rules and gives you some assurance of the quality of your reference.

If a writer does not wish to provide you with a copy of the letter, don't insist upon it.   Academic references are still mostly confidential, although the tide is turning very slowly towards full disclosure.   This is a startling contrast to the business world, where copying the candidate on a letter of reference is standard practice and a professional courtesy.

e. **Format.**   Letters from your professors should be professionally typed and printed on the school's stationary. Other letters you request may not automatically come in this form. If at all possible, ask your writers to send the letters typed on professional letterhead with a laser-jet or inkjet printer.   For some business schools, the writers are not asked to submit a general letter, but to answer several specific questions.   If this is the case, you should tailor your list of Match Points to address the specific questions that are asked by each school.   (We will discuss this extensively in Chapter 5).

f. **Organization.**   Organize the forms, envelopes, program descriptions, and other materials you will give to each reference writer in a logical manner.   One simple technique is to paper-clip the form, program description, and the school's envelope together.   Then, to make sure they remain together, place them in a large padded envelope; write your name, the writer's name and the date the letters are due on the outside of the padded envelope. Remember that you will have to create a separate padded envelope for each person who is writing a reference letter for you.

When you complete Appendix 2 (your request for reference letters), list the schools in chronological order, with the earliest deadlines first. The chronological list makes it easy for faculty members to complete your letters of recommendation on time.

g. **Follow-up**. Two weeks after a writer agrees to send the reference letter, verify that it has reached its destination. If it hasn't, ask him/her to send a second copy. Then, send a thank-you note to each person who took the time to write a letter on your behalf; it not only shows good manners, but will encourage the writer to continue to offer references for future applicants.   A terrific example of a thank-you letter is included in Appendix 4.

Your final step, which is often overlooked by busy applicants, is to notify your authors of the final admissions decision. Use the opportunity to re-thank them for their continual support of your career.   It is never too soon to build your professional network.

h. **If Asked to Write Your Own**. In some cases, the people you ask to write your recommendation letters may be too busy to tackle the job.   Instead, they will instruct you to write the letter yourself and simply submit it back to them for a signature. Most applicants consider this a dream come true. After all, what could be better than a chance to "toot your own horn" under the guise of being your own boss or major professor?

Sadly, most candidates haven't a clue what an excellent reference letter looks like. To assume the perspective and tone of someone in your recommender's position requires a considerable amount of experience. Most letters written by the actual candidates are embarrassingly easy to spot: they include far too many details that a real reference letter wouldn't mention and they are identical in tone to the candidate's own writing.

We strongly discourage you from trying to write your own letters. Remember, the admissions committee has viewed thousands of letters and has a good eye for what a real recommendation does – and does NOT – say.   There are also moral and ethical considerations with writing your own letters.   Business schools do not want to admit sneaky candidates who bend the rules to suit their own whim; they want ethical candidates who are willing to obtain an honest appraisal of their credentials from an objective, well qualified third party. Instead of trying to write your own letters, give the author a copy of your Match Points (Appendix 3), which summarizes your fit for your program of choice.   Ask him/her to elaborate on those points to complete the letter.   If (s)he refuses, ask someone else, who is willing to take the time to write a reference that genuinely reflects your suitability for the program to which you are applying.

Chapter 5:   How to Write a Persuasive Reference Letter

Assume for a moment that you've just been asked to write your first reference letter.   If you are like most people, you were totally flattered by the request.   After all, when a candidate asks you to recommend him/her for business school, it implies that you are an expert on the subject;   you know what it takes to succeed at a competitive MBA program.   But that doesn't necessarily mean that you are in a position to endorse the particular candidate who has asked you.   Before you agree to write a letter, you must have a frank discussion with the candidate about your ability to fulfill his/her expectations.

A.   Establish honestly and directly whether or not you can write a positive letter on behalf of the applicant.   If you only have limited knowledge of the person's talents (or a negative impression of him/her), then you cannot in good conscience provide a positive letter.   From our experience, an ambiguous or lukewarm reference can cause as much harm as a negative one.   Tell the candidate your concerns upfront.   Although the conversation may be awkward, it will enable the applicant to address whatever issues you may have.   Alternatively, the candidate may decide to pursue a more enthusiastic person to write a letter on his/her behalf.

Note: From our perspective, the most gracious ways to decline a request are to say that you:

1.   do not have enough time to do an effective job
2.   are not familiar enough with a candidate's work or background to do him/her justice
3.   do not have the credibility to impress the committee at that particular school/program

In all cases, try to suggest someone else who can do a better job on the candidate's behalf.   By keeping the emphasis on delivering the best letter possible, you can minimize any hurt feelings.

When deciding whether or not to write a letter, remember that your reputation is at stake.   If you work in academia (and write numerous reference letters), admissions officers will eventually become familiar with what you have said about other candidates.   If you routinely oversell the applicants (or over-inflate their capabilities), after a few years, no one will believe what you say.   The best way to retain your credibility is to be highly selective in whom you choose to support.   You will write fewer recommendations, but they will be more meaningful in the selection process.

B.   If you agree to write a letter to support the candidate, you must maintain the integrity of the process by personally writing the letter, rather than simply signing a draft that the candidate has already written.   However, soliciting ideas from the candidate regarding the focus and content of the letter is not only acceptable, but recommended.

C. Give the candidate a copy of **a Reference Letter Request Form** (Appendix 5), which summarizes all of the information you will need to write the letter.   At the very least, you should have a copy of the candidate's:

1.   Resume
2.   Personal Statement
3.   Statement of Goals
4.   Match Points (Appendix 3)
5.   Written permission for you to send a reference letter on his/her behalf (Appendix 2)
6.   A complete list of all schools to which the letter should be sent, along with the deadlines for each (Appendix 2)

D.   Before putting pen to paper, be sure to review your organization's policy regarding letters of recommendation. Since most letters are printed on corporate letterhead, many firms have rigid guidelines in place to protect themselves against potential lawsuits. The common rule is to write only positive, factual recommendation letters that refrain from any type of derogatory remarks. If you cannot adhere to this requirement, you should decline the candidate's request.

Organizing the Letter

As a general rule, reference letters include four distinct parts:

1. An **introduction**, which explains who you are, your relationship to the candidate and why you feel qualified to assess his/her suitability for the program.   Explain how long you have known the applicant and in what capacity. State your qualifications for writing the recommendation letter. Why should the reader be interested in your

perspective? How many other people of the applicant's caliber have you known; why does the applicant stand out?

2.   A **discussion of the candidate's strengths** and how they relate to the needs of the program.   Discuss the applicant's exceptional qualities and skills, especially those that are relevant in a business career.   As a first step, review the general categories of skills that we presented in Chapter 3. Include your own observations of the candidate's strengths, along with the list of Match Points that the candidate has provided. These observations will form the foundation of your reference letter.

We recommend that authors organize their discussion of the candidate's strengths in the following manner:

a.   First, provide a *general assessment of the applicant's performance* and potential for career growth, in the context in which you know him/her.   If the applicant was your student, mention how well (s)he did in your classes and the particular skills (s)he used to accomplish this.   If the candidate is your employee, discuss how well (s)he executes his/her job responsibilities.   Highlight the applicant's key accomplishments and strengths.

b.   Next, discuss the candidate's *oral and written communication skills*.   Highlight any publications or presentations you have observed.

c.   Discuss the candidate's *maturity level and interpersonal skills*.   Highlight exceptional personal strengths, including how well the candidate gets along with others and his/her level of reliability and responsibility.

d.   Finally, discuss any *special skills or strengths* the candidate may possess, such as language fluencies, multicultural expertise or a commitment to volunteer work.

For each characteristic or trait that you mention, give specific examples or anecdotes to support what you say.   In reference letters, the power is in the details; generalized praise is not particularly helpful.

3.   A **comparison** of the candidate to others who have succeeded in business school.   Give your judgment of the applicant, his/her qualifications and potential. Why should (s)he be considered over other candidates? How does (s)he compare to other MBA candidates you have known?   Write only complimentary (yet factual) observations.

If asked to discuss a candidate's flaws or weaknesses, choose something that can be presented as an opportunity for growth (we offer several suggestions later in this chapter).   The best choices are traits that the candidate has already taken steps to correct, such as a lack of knowledge or training in a particular area.   Avoid unflattering or derogatory remarks.

4.   A **conclusion**, which summarizes the candidate's outstanding strengths and abilities.   Offer a strong ending, but don't overdo it.   Excessive praise can be viewed as biased or insincere.   Finally, list your contact information if you are willing to respond to follow-up correspondence.

Chapter 6 - 15 provide several samples of successful reference letters for business school, which use different approaches to convey the applicant's unique strengths.   Use the letters as inspiration for your own original writing.

Free-Style Letters vs. Question & Answer Format

Business schools, more than any other type of graduate program, prefer that reference writers answer a list of questions about the applicant, rather than submit a free-style letter.   Most top-tier programs have their own form to complete, which captures the writer's thoughts on the candidate's accomplishments and strengths.

Unfortunately, this approach is extremely time intensive; if a candidate applies to six programs, (s)he will need for each of his/her reference writers to complete six separate forms, with differing questions and length restrictions. From our experience, few authors have the time to do this.   As a result, it is not unusual for authors to simply send all of the schools *one general letter* that provides a comprehensive evaluation of the candidate.

From working in admissions, I understand both sides of this dilemma.   From the school's standpoint, the questionnaire targets the specific issues that they want to know about; it also imposes a rigid length requirement to focus the author on the most relevant issues.   In a free-style letter, there is no guarantee that the author will cover the essential points in an efficient manner.   From the writer's perspective, a questionnaire removes some of the ambiguity of writing a reference letter by providing the structure and focus that the school expects.

Otherwise, the questionnaires are strictly for the school's benefit, not the reference writer's. Because the questions and length restrictions vary among schools, writers cannot always use the answers they wrote for one school for a second or third one. Frequently, the job requires significant "cutting and pasting" to answer one question without overlapping the answer to a different question. And for schools with rigid length restrictions, a lot of critical information may be lost in the editing process. Our best advice:

1. As a *candidate*, try to do everything possible to make the job easier for your writers. Read through the questions on each school's form and target your Match Points to address each one. This will maximize the chances of the writer using the questionnaires, rather than submitting a general letter.

2. As a *writer*, organize the questionnaires and coordinate your answers before you begin to write. If at all possible, answer all of the questions directly on the school's form. If you absolutely, positively cannot take the time to do this, advise the candidate at the time that (s)he gives you the forms. Let him/her decide whether or not (s)he is comfortable with your decision to write a general letter.

If you opt to write a general letter, make sure that it addresses *all* of the points on *all* of the forms. If you find it helpful, use titles for each section of the letter, such as "key strengths," "communication skills," "team work," and "weaknesses." Print your letter on official letterhead, sign it in ink and attach it to the school's questionnaire (which you should also sign in ink). As long as the letter is concise, on-topic and well-written, it will suffice.

Chapters 6 – 15 offer multiple examples of both the questionnaire approach and the use of free-style letters. As you will see, both can be highly effective.

Writing Guidelines

1. As a rule of thumb, the "correct" length for a reference letter is one or two typewritten pages. You should include enough information to supplement the committee's impression of the candidate, without overwhelming the reader with details that are unrelated to the application.

2. Focus on qualitative information, rather than quantitative. By the time the admissions committee reads your letter, they will have already reviewed the candidate's transcripts and GMAT scores. Rather than repeat those details, you should share your "behind the scenes" insight into the candidate's performance and his/her potential to succeed in business school. To whatever extent possible, you should give the committee positive information about the candidate that they could not acquire any other way.

3. Read the candidate's application essays to get an idea of the strengths that (s)he is trying to convey to the committee. Ideally, your letter will *complement* (and build upon) the information the candidate has provided in his/her essays without *duplicating* it.

4. Offer a balanced perspective of the candidate. Admissions committees appreciate letters that offer honest assessments, including areas for growth; they do not expect perfection.

5. Do not make any statements that you cannot support with facts and examples. Do not editorialize or speculate. If you give an opinion, explain the incident or circumstances upon which you are basing it. Be able to document all of the information that you release. To avoid a possible claim of defamation, do not comment about the candidate's moral character.

6. Write with enthusiasm. Use powerful words, such as articulate, effective, intelligent, significant, creative, efficient, cooperative, assertive, dependable, mature and innovative. Avoid bland words such as nice, reasonable, decent, fairly and satisfactory. Although they may seem perfectly fine to you, in admissions circles, they scream "average" or "mediocre."

7. If there are extenuating circumstances that have impacted the candidate's academic or professional progress, you should obtain the candidate's written permission to disclose that information. Business schools value the perspective of someone who knows an applicant well, especially in reference to possible challenges that (s)he has overcome. Nevertheless, these topics (such as homelessness, divorce, or illness) should NOT be discussed in your letter without the candidate's express written permission.

8. Do **not** reveal any information that could be viewed as discriminatory, including the candidate's race, color, religion, national origin, political affiliation, age, disability, sexual orientation, physical appearance, citizenship status or marital status.

9. If you are an alumnus of the school to which the candidate is applying (or have completed a similar program), feel free to elaborate on the applicant's fit for that particular program.   Explain how (s)he will add to the student body and be a good role model.

10. Type your letter on official letterhead and sign it in ink.   A professional presentation will reflect positively on the candidate.   Handwritten letters are not only difficult to read, but detract markedly from the writer's credibility.   Sadly, admissions committees rarely take the time to read them.

11. If a candidate asks you to address a letter "to whom it may concern," note that in the body of the letter.   Also note that the candidate has agreed to take responsibility for disseminating the letter to the proper person.

12. If your company has concerns about liability issues regarding reference letters, include the following sentence at the end of your letter:

"This information is provided at the request of [name of applicant], who has asked me to serve as a reference.   My comments are confidential and should be treated as such.   They reflect my own opinions about the candidate's suitability for business school.   No other use or inference is intended."

This type of disclaimer explains the purpose of your letter and confirms that it was not written to hurt the applicant's reputation.

13. Ask the candidate to let you know the committee's decision.

14. Keep a copy of every letter you send – and document when you sent it.   This information will come in handy if, for whatever reason, the letter does not reach its destination (and must be re-sent).

Explaining Weaknesses

For most authors, the trickiest part of writing a reference letter is discussing a candidate's "weaknesses" or "areas of development."   Few writers want to document an applicant's faults on record, for both personal and legal reasons. Nevertheless, the BEST recommendations give a balanced perspective of the applicant, including a brief assessment of the areas in which (s)he can improve.   If you omit this section, or offer an insincere reply, your letter will lose a portion of its integrity.

From our perspective, the best weaknesses to mention fall into three categories:

1. Areas that the candidate is already working on

Examples:

A poor public speaker who improves his/her skills by joining Toastmasters
Someone with no computer skills who takes a programming class
A candidate who joins a professional association to expand his/her network

2. Areas that will be addressed through the graduate program to which (s)he is applying

Examples:

A candidate with no international experience who applies to a program overseas
A successful paralegal who cannot advance in the profession without a law degree

3. Positive personality traits that need to be tempered

Examples:

A candidate who works 24/7, to the detriment of his/her personal life
A candidate who needs to reign in his/her sense of humor
A candidate who is overly detail oriented, but misses the big picture
A perfectionist who delivers top quality work, but takes forever to do it

Weaknesses that are Deal Breakers.

From our perspective, mentioning the following "weaknesses" will sabotage the candidate's application, and may leave the writer in a legal quagmire. In these situations, you should decline to write a reference on the person's behalf:

a. candidates who have committed immoral, illegal or unethical acts
b. candidates who cannot get along with other people
c. candidates who are incompetent in their current jobs
d. candidates with difficult personalities

No matter how clever you try to be, the committee will "read between the lines" to try to decipher what you AREN'T saying.

Examples:	Sharon marches to her own beat, which few other students hear.
	Because she is fiercely independent, Sharon excels at working alone.
	Rather than participate in campus events, Sharon prefers to keep to herself.
Translation:	Sharon is a misfit who is NOT a team player. She has low leadership potential.
Examples:	In a few years, when he matures, Brad will undoubtedly fulfill his potential.
	Regardless of the circumstances, Brad is always the life of the party.
	After a slow start, Brad managed to complete his term paper.
	Brad's speech, although short on content, was slick and polished.
Translation:	Brad is a funny guy who is hopelessly immature. He's not ready for this commitment.

Common Problems in Reference Letters

Here are the most common problems we observe in reference letters. If at all possible, avoid sending letters that:

a. are typed on plain paper instead of letterhead.

b. do not include the writer's signature and/or contact information.

c. do not include the confidentiality waiver for the letter (sometimes, students forget to give the form to the writer; other times, the writer forgets to return the form to the school).

d. contain unsupported, over-enthusiastic or generic endorsements, instead of offering useful, balanced insights.

e. concentrate on the writer and/or the class, with only a brief reference to the student.

f. disclose personal and controversial information about the applicant that does not enhance his/her candidacy, including personal or political views.

g. contain school-specific or company-specific jargon that is unfamiliar to the admissions committee. If in doubt, show the material to an intelligent person whose formal education is in a different field. If (s)he cannot understand it, the committee probably won't, either. And, sad to say, they won't be impressed by something they can't understand.

Helpful Phrases for Reference Letters

Chapters 6 - 15 provide numerous examples of successful reference letters for business school. We encourage you to use them as inspiration for your own original writing. As you will see, there are several universal statements that are incumbent in all reference letters. If you aren't sure how to get started, or are struggling with writer's block, consider the following phrases as guidelines:

1. Opening Statements

I am writing this letter at the request of Jane Smith, who is an applicant for your business school class.

I am pleased to write this letter of recommendation for Jane Smith.

Please accept this letter as my enthusiastic endorsement of Jane Smith.

My name is Tom James and I am a Manager at Bank One. I am delighted to write a letter of reference for Jane Smith to support her application to business school.

2. Your Qualifications to Evaluate the Candidate

In my 20-year teaching career, I have advised approximately 450 students on independent research projects.

I have personally supervised ten interns every summer for the last five years as a trainer for Bank One.

In my career at Rice University, I have seen hundreds of undergraduate students seek admission to business school.

In over ten years as the CEO of Infotech, I have supervised 50 other programmers with Jane's education and experience.

3. How well you know the Candidate

I know Jane well, because she attended two of my sections every week, although only one was required.

Mark reported directly to me for two years prior to his well-deserved promotion to Manager at Bell South.

We enjoyed several after-class discussions about Jane's research, which offered fascinating preliminary results.

I was delighted when Rita asked me to be her advisor for her senior literature project.

4. Candidate's Greatest Strengths

Rachel has the rare blend of analytical and interpersonal skills that a finance career requires.

Rachel is the hardest working, most tenacious engineer I have ever known.

Rachel was one of the most productive, caring and effective nurses I have had the pleasure of knowing.

Rachel's greatest talent is fundraising on behalf of cancer research.

5. Assessment Statements

John is an enthusiastic self-starter with an impressive command of technology.

Despite the competing demands on her time, Alexis consistently produced high quality work in a timely fashion.

By using a highly creative approach, Carter quickly re-defined our expectations of a good project manager.

In his four years with us, Ben has completed four of my classes and has been one of our most successful undergraduate students.

6. Evidence to Support a Strength

Jake is the only student who came to all of my office hours to master financial theory. He was one of only two students to receive an A in the course.

Because of Jane's writing skills, I asked her to write a research report for a major policy decision. Based on Jane's sophisticated 20-page analysis of airborne contaminants, Congressman Jones lobbied the State for additional funding.

Jane's technological and quantitative skills are exemplary; the various scheduling, work-flow and asset management software systems that she developed contained complicated algorithms that are beyond the scope of most developers.

After the Supreme Court's examination of racial discrimination/affirmative action in law school admission at the University of Michigan, Fran produced a thorough and well-written analysis of the decision, which argued at length in support of Justice Clarence Thomas's dissenting opinion.

7. Rating or Ranking Statements

Jane was in the top 10% of her class.

Zachary has the best analytical skills of any chemist I have ever supervised.

Rachel is in the top 5% of all students I have seen, both in academic achievement and practical skills.

As a teacher, I treasure the rare student who has the talent and skill to make a significant contribution to his field.   Zane is one of those rare students.

8. Mild Criticism / Presenting a Weakness

John's only fault is his retiring nature. His modesty sometimes hides his remarkable strengths.

Julie's persistence can turn into stubbornness, but her good nature ultimately prevails.

With training in finance, Carl will be better prepared to evaluate projects from a business perspective.

The only area of weakness that I ever noted in Jane's performance was her minimal background in statistics.   Fortunately, she is now taking a class at the community college to remedy this deficiency.

9. Candidate's Potential for Success

I enthusiastically recommend David to your business school. This passionate, well-rounded student will be an extraordinary leader.

With her exceptional leadership, writing and quantitative skills, Sondra will be a credit to whatever business school she attends.

George's leadership potential is superb.

I am confident that Joe will be an asset to student life at Harvard Business School.

10. Closing Statements

I am pleased to recommend John for admission to business school.

Based on my time working with Susan, I recommend her very highly for a business school of Harvard's caliber.

In summary, I am pleased to recommend Jose without reservation.

From my observation, Zachary will undoubtedly succeed at whatever business school he chooses.

General Traits To Emphasize

Depending on your relationship with the candidate, the committee will have different expectations of what they expect your letter to say. As a general rule, these are the traits that are most highly prized in the admissions process.

Remember, when you draft your letter, you should restrict your comments to your actual interactions with the candidate – and the achievements *you have actually observed*. Anything that you've "heard" about the candidate from a third party, regardless of how flattering, will be regarded as hearsay if you repeat it in your recommendation letter.

Academic Strengths

Intelligence
Scholarship
Analytical skills
Reasoning skills
Curiosity
Mastery of specific subject area

Innovative
Insightful
Creative
Well-rounded
Class participation
Observant

Professional Strengths

Leadership skills
Hard-working
Motivated
Tenacious
Ambitious
Self-starter
Creative
Resourceful
Efficient
Good manager
Writing skills
Presentation skills
Strong interpersonal skills

Versatile
Ethical
Independent
Well organized
Planning skills
Technical skills (be specific)
Attention to detail
High energy level
Communication skills
Attentive listener
Perseverance
Good judgment
Negotiation skills

Personal / Interpersonal Strengths

Friendly
Optimistic
Polite
Well-mannered
Mature
Team player
Patient
Kind
Empathetic

Loyal
Sincere
Modest
Sense of integrity
Reliable
Flexible
Generous
Assertive

Chapter 6: Letters from Professors

Nearly every business school requires candidates to send a recommendation letter from an undergraduate faculty member.   Ideally, the author should be a full-time professor in a tenure-track position at his/her school, with one of the following titles/rankings: Assistant Professor, Associate Professor, Professor, or Dean.

If possible, avoid sending letters from teaching assistants, Ph.D. candidates, or adjunct faculty members, regardless of how enthusiastic they may be.   From an admissions standpoint, authors in these positions do not have the perspective they need to compare you to other business school candidates.   Consequently, their claims will not be given adequate weight in the decision-making process.

As we discussed in Chapter 2, the "perfect" professor to write your letter is someone who:

a.   understands the intellectual demands of business school
b.   knows you well enough to evaluate your qualifications
c.   is willing/able to provide enough supporting detail to justify his/her assessment

In paragraph 1: the author should explain his/her relationship with you, including:

His/her title
How long (s)he has known you
How many classes you have completed with him/her
The titles of those classes
Any outside interactions (s)he has had with you
The nature of those outside interactions (example: research advisor)

In paragraph 2 (and possibly 3):   the author should briefly state his/her overall impression of you as a student.   Then, (s)he should mention the specific qualities that you demonstrated in his/her classroom.   Bear in mind, whether you are writing a letter or requesting one for yourself, the power is in the details.   Do not simply mention the grade the candidate earned in the class.   Instead, take the time to document the specific talents or skills the person demonstrated to earn that grade.

For example, in science and math classes, students must use their analytical and quantitative skills to solve practical problems.   Professors in these classes should document the candidate's critical thinking skills; if the professor supervised a laboratory class, (s)he should also document the candidate's mastery of scientific principles and various analytical methods.

Likewise, students who major in journalism, English, education, and business are expected to be excellent communicators.   Professors from these disciplines should provide an objective assessment of the candidate's ability to speak and write in a clear, logical, and persuasive manner.

Finally, artistic students, such as writers, painters, and musicians, are usually creative and independent thinkers who have the confidence to express themselves through their work.   Professors should document the talent they have developed over time.

Regardless of the candidate's background, the author should focus on *one or two exceptional traits* that (s)he has personally observed that person demonstrate in the classroom.   The letter should document those strengths and offer a specific example to support the praise.

For example, if a letter claims that a candidate is a good writer, the author must mention a specific paper or assignment that the candidate completed in an extraordinary way.   What was the topic? The length?   What was terrific about the paper – was it short, concise, well documented, or unusually insightful?   Be specific.

In the next paragraph: All students, regardless of their background or major, are expected to demonstrate a strong love of learning and the appropriate level of respect for their fellow students.   Authors should document these points in the following paragraph, by mentioning the candidate's participation in class, willingness to help others, and attendance at office hours.   If appropriate, the author should also document the candidate's ability to work in a team environment.   Is (s)he a natural leader?   Did (s)he pull his/her weight on any class projects or presentations?   If so, offer specific details.

In the penultimate paragraph: mention any other notable facts about the candidate that you want to convey. This section of the letter has the most flexibility, depending upon the candidate's background and what you have personally observed. Good points to include:

a. Participation in outside activities related the candidate's major (or a business career)
b. Entrepreneurial ventures the candidate has launched
c. Practical experience in the candidate's major, through internships, summer work, or paid employment
d. The ability to succeed in the face of adversity. As we discussed in Chapter 5, this can be tricky if the candidate does not want you to reveal the information. Nevertheless, there are situations in which the committee cannot properly assess the candidate's character and motivation unless they know the whole story.

From our perspective, the following factors are worth mentioning:

a. The candidate earned excellent grades while working full-time to support himself/herself.
b. The candidate graduated on time, despite suffering a life-threatening illness or injury.
c. The candidate has documented learning disabilities, but did not request special accommodations in the classroom (or for the GMAT).
d. The candidate was a top performer, despite wrestling with serious personal challenges at home (divorce, death, familial illness, language or cultural barriers).

Although these issues are private – and deeply difficult to talk about – the way a candidate deals with them is an indication of his/her maturity and character. If you have the applicant's permission to mention the issue – and you are willing to do so – you can provide the committee with insight into the candidate's life that they could not acquire any other way.

In the final paragraph: put your opinion of the candidate into the proper perspective. How many students have you taught in your entire career? How does the candidate compare to that group – the top 1%, 5%, or 20%? If you have specific experience with students who have obtained an MBA, it is particularly helpful to compare the candidate to that group. If the applicant is equally intelligent, motivated, and dynamic, this is the place to mention it.

In the closing statement: offer a brief summary of the candidate's qualifications and state the strength of your recommendation (enthusiastic, without reservation, etc.). In the last sentence, you should provide your contact information (phone number and email address) in case the committee wants to confirm your letter or acquire additional details. Although it is highly unlikely that someone will contact you, your letter will have an added level of credibility if you indicate that you are receptive to further contact.

Finally, print your letter on your official letterhead and sign it as follows:

John Smith, Ph.D.   (Name, Academic Degree)
Professor of English   (Formal Title)
Harvard University   (Affiliation)

Here are several recommendation letters for business school candidates that were written by seasoned faculty members. To protect the privacy of the writer and applicant, the names of all people, classes, schools, places, and companies have been changed.

Letter #1: From Professor

I am pleased to write this letter of recommendation for Valerie Douglas, who I taught for four years at New York University. As part of her BA degree in Literature, she completed two of my writing classes and impressed me in a number of ways.

Valerie's talent as a writer is exceeded only by her enthusiasm. In my Intermediate Fiction class, she became increasingly excited about the course material as the semester progressed. Although she initially avoided the science fiction genre, Valerie's final short story, "Escape from Babylon," was simply brilliant. In addition to creating likeable characters and a suspenseful plot, Valerie displayed a gift for dialogue, along with a subtle flair for black comedy. Without her knowledge, I submitted the story to *Tremors Digest* for publication. They featured it in their August 2009 issue.

I was delighted when Valerie asked me to be her advisor for her senior literature project. Taking a break from fiction, she opted to do a survey piece on the effects of the 9/11 terrorist attacks on inner city children. The paper required extensive research, including several dozen interviews with students and teachers in the heart of New York City. Rather than scale down her project, Valerie worked nights and weekends to ensure its timely completion. Throughout the project, Valerie proved to be a good listener and insightful interviewer. Her final draft captures both the innocence of the children and their vague awareness of how life had changed since the loss of the World Trade Center.

In the summer of 2008, Valerie demonstrated her strong analytical, critiquing and writing skills in my Early Classics Seminar. Among other assignments, she wrote two strong papers about the Bronte sisters and collaborated with three of her classmates on a skillfully written "period novella." On our final day of class, Valerie led a well-prepared and professionally delivered group presentation that showed her deep knowledge of English literature.

Throughout her undergraduate career, Valerie consistently demonstrated the following skills, abilities and characteristics:

- Successfully plans and completes long-term projects, including comprehensive papers and manuscripts
- Interacts effectively with a wide variety of people, including her professors, peers, and interview subjects
- Shows initiative, creativity and persistence in difficult situations
- Speaks and writes clearly and persuasively

In summary, I am pleased to recommend Valerie Douglas to you without reservation. If you have any questions regarding her application, please don't hesitate to call me at 555-555-5555.

Our Assessment: This professor, who was one of Valerie's college mentors, provides valuable insight into her early achievements as a published author. The reader learns that Valerie has always been a passionate writer with a gift for personal narrative. When considered in conjunction with her other recommendations, which documented her subsequent success in the world of publishing, this letter confirmed that Valerie has always been a woman of character and ambition.

Letter #2: From Professor

My name is Dr. Lisa Sanders and I am a Professor of Chemistry at Harvard University.   I am delighted to write a letter of reference for Gloria Smith to support her application to business school.

I have known Gloria for four years through her work at the university.   Gloria completed three of my classes (Chemistry I & II, Analytical Chemistry) and achieved "A" grades in each.   She also distinguished herself as a highly motivated and talented scientist.   Most of our students are challenged to complete our traditional program in chemistry and wouldn't dream of attempting a dual major.   Gloria willingly accepted the opportunity.   She graduated from Harvard in 2009 with a dual major in Chemistry and Genetic Biology.   In addition to attaining high academic honors, Gloria also excelled in her laboratory work.   To date, she has published two articles on the effects of reduced salt intake on weight loss in obese children.   Throughout her coursework and independent research, Gloria was always organized, cheerful and willing to help others.   She demonstrated excellent potential for a career in the sciences.

Gloria's research success was partially attributable to her strong interpersonal skills.   She works well with all types of people and quickly puts others at ease.   A huge challenge in her research was explaining the diet and exercise protocol to the participating children and their families.   Gloria quickly established a positive rapport with all 50 subjects and their parents.   She patiently answered their questions and encouraged the children who were ambivalent about participating.   Long after the completion of the study, Gloria continued to keep in touch with several families via email to offer encouraging tips to promote further weight loss.   I am certain that the project would not have been successful without her graciousness and dedication.

I am also impressed by Gloria's initiative outside the classroom.   During her sophomore year, she started a small internet/mail order business selling hand-painted T-shirts.   She researched the field on her own and did all of the web design work herself.   At first, I was surprised that Gloria took on such a venture, but she thrived under the bustling schedule.   Her shirts were extremely popular on campus; I often saw her selling them from a small booth she set up outside our student union.   I initially chuckled at Gloria's creative way to earn a few dollars on the side.   I later discovered that the business netted almost $70,000 during its first year, which covered her tuition and expenses.

I had to marvel at Gloria's initiative, organizational skills and willingness to take risks.   During her senior year, she also became an employer, as she expanded her business to the local state university in Framingham.   In this capacity, Gloria developed many practical skills in marketing, manufacturing, web site design, advertising, payroll and time management.   I am certain that this success is only the first of many for her.

In my career at Harvard, I have seen hundreds of undergraduates seek advanced degrees in the sciences.   It isn't often that I am asked to write a reference letter for a scientist who wants to pursue a business degree.   I am delighted to support Gloria's efforts to pursue a career that will combine her analytical strengths and her practical business skills.   She recently told me that her long-term goal was to own a biotechnology firm that conducts international biogenetic research.   I wouldn't doubt her for a minute.   Gloria is in the top 5% of all students I have known, both in academic achievement and practical skills.   She will be a tremendous addition to your class.

Our Assessment: This author is a noted professor at Harvard who rarely writes such strong letters of support.   Her detailed explanation of Gloria's strengths in science and business, including her impressive entrepreneurial success, made a positive impression on the committee.

Letter #3: From Finance Professor

I am pleased to write this recommendation on behalf of Savannah Stevens, who was a student in the finance program at Stanford University between 2004 and 2008. I taught her in two classes and also served as Department Head for the duration of her undergraduate program. During that time, I watched Savannah mature into a poised and accomplished young woman with excellent work habits and superior interpersonal skills. She remains one of my favorite students.

From her first days in my Options & Derivatives class, Savannah demonstrated incomparable diligence, analytical skills and an ability to think on her feet. The class tends to be particularly challenging because a major portion of the grade is based on class presentations. Every week, students were asked to research a series of investment products (stocks, bonds, options, mutual funds, etc.) and to select the one most likely to achieve a specific financial goal. On any given day, students were randomly selected to defend their choices in class. Savannah was an excellent researcher who understood how to apply basic information to specific scenarios. More impressively, she handled difficult (sometimes hostile) questions from her fellow students with grace and confidence. Even when her choice deviated from the "correct" answer, Savannah demonstrated excellent reasoning skills in selecting and defending her choice. She consistently maintained her poise and sense of humor while other students were reduced to tears.

For her senior project in finance, Savannah developed and managed an investment club at a local retirement community. Savannah's job was to recruit the participants and explain the risk/reward profile of various investment options. Throughout the semester, Savannah did an exceptional job explaining the different stock sectors to 36 novice investors. She patiently answered questions, discussed brokerage house options, and taught the participants how to research their picks on the Internet. The group not only made money; they had great fun. Throughout the semester, I watched Savannah become more confident in her ability to manage a challenging project. The investment club was an unqualified success, largely because of her dedication.

In addition to her academic success in our rigorous finance program, Savannah is also a talented vocalist with strong ties to community theatre. In late 2007, while performing in "Don Giovanni," Savannah became fascinated by the short story upon which the opera was based. We enjoyed several after-class discussions about the work, whose meaning is often debated by seasoned literary critics. Savannah became intrigued by the work's subtleties, noting that its interpretation depended upon the language in which it was read; the French to English translation of specific words created considerable ambiguity. After reading the French version of the story, Savannah wrote a superb analysis of the compromises inherent in the English translation. Her essay was flawless, including a logical and insightful analysis. The paper remains a crown jewel in the English literature department.

Savannah is a motivated young woman of numerous talents and considerable self-discipline. Whether studying derivative curves, writing an essay, or preparing for an operatic performance, she gives each endeavor her full focus and attention. This passion and determination are rare and precious gifts.

In over twenty-five years of teaching, I have known few other students with Savannah's talent and drive. I am certain that she will be an asset to student life at XXXXXXX Business School.

Our Assessment: This letter was written by a well-known professor at Stanford University. Its strength is that the author clearly knows the applicant well and is favorably impressed by her work. The writer did a great job of citing specific examples of Savannah's financial expertise and community service work. She also documented the candidate's unusual skills as a vocalist and writer. By citing Savannah's tenacity and discipline, she distinguished her from the hundreds of other applicants with similar academic achievements.

Letter #4: From Professor

I am honored to write a letter of recommendation on behalf of Ms. Daphne Ling, who has applied for admission to XXX Business School.   In 2007, Daphne completed my course entitled The Psychology of Post-Traumatic Stress Disorder (PTSD) at Princeton University.   Her exemplary performance in the class, combined with her passion, maturity, and insight, confirmed her ability to succeed at a school of XXX's caliber.

Over the course of the term, the students discussed several situations in which patients experienced PTSD; they also investigated the most popular treatment modalities, including drug therapy, biofeedback, and mental health counseling.   Daphne excelled in all aspects of the course, including a term paper on the long-term effects of sexual abuse on children.   This topic was dear to Daphne's heart, because she had endured a similar type of abuse at the hands of a day care worker.   In her class presentation, Daphne discussed her experience in an honest and expressive manner, including her current work as a peer therapist for other victims of sexual abuse.   Daphne's wiliness to reveal this information greatly enhanced the class's understanding of PTSD.   They also appreciated her courage and strength under such difficult circumstances.   In my many years of teaching, I have rarely encountered a more persuasive or insightful undergraduate student.

At the end of the course term, Daphne gave a 30-minute presentation on the topic of bravery.   Rather than repeat someone else's thoughts on the subject, Daphne interviewed several people in New Orleans, who had miraculously re-built their lives after Hurricane Katrina.   For her presentation, Daphne created a videotape that summarized the many obstacles they faced to rebuild their homes and lives after the flood had receded.   For this moving project, which comprised 50% of her course grade, Daphne revealed an extraordinary level of compassion, organization and insight. She also gave her classmates food for thought on what it meant to be "brave."   As her professor, I am impressed by her willingness to think "outside the box" and make intelligent, well-reasoned decisions.   In honor of her work, Daphne received the highest mark in the class, which was a well-deserved achievement.

Without a doubt, Daphne's greatest strength is her natural affinity as a speaker, which has sparked her impressive achievements inside and outside the classroom.   In 2007, our department hired Daphne as a Teaching Assistant for third-year courses that are usually assigned to graduate students, such as Abnormal Psychology and Grief, Death & Bereavement.   By assuming this role, Daphne became an excellent speaker who could convey technical information in an enjoyable and understandable way.   Her experience as a teacher and researcher will enable her to make an immediate contribution to your program.

In my twenty-year career as an educator, I have worked with thousands of intelligent and talented students.   Few have impressed me as positively as Daphne Ling.   Her maturity, determination, and exemplary work ethic, combined with her delightful personal qualities, have made her an extraordinary student.   If given a chance, she will undoubtedly accomplish great feats at XXX Business School.

Our Assessment: This professor not only documented Daphne's skills as a student, speaker, and researcher, but as a survivor who used her own experience to help others. As a result, the reader learned what a strong and exceptional woman Daphne was – and the many positive traits she would bring to her MBA studies.

Letter #5:   From Literary Professor

How long have you known the applicant and in what capacity?

I am pleased to recommend Elizabeth Barrington for admission to your institution. I have known Elizabeth for three years as a student in my creative writing classes.   During that time, she proved to be a creative, industrious and prolific writer.

What is the applicant's greatest strength?   Please give an example.

In the classroom, Elizabeth was a joy to work with. She constantly strove to produce innovative manuscripts about the real-life challenges of women.   In my Creative Fiction III class, I encouraged Elizabeth to submit her work to the mainstream press.   By the end of the semester, Elizabeth had four short stories accepted for publication in national magazines.   Her future in creative writing is whatever she chooses to make it.

Outside the classroom, Elizabeth has lent her writing and editing skills to several volunteer organizations, including the Seattle chapter of Amnesty International.   In 2007, Elizabeth authored a twelve-page brochure that described their mission and goals.   She also scripted their commercials for local television.   As expected, her material was well written, well organized and well received in the community.   I admire her willingness to lend her skills to a group that she is passionate about.

By actively seeking opportunities to write, including freelance assignments for national magazines, Elizabeth already earns her living as a published author.   She is an inspiration to other students and faculty members who "can't find the time" to pursue their own projects.   On several occasions, Elizabeth has graciously offered to help her fellow students with their manuscripts.   In our 2008 summer creative writing conference, she demonstrated excellent project management skills in compiling a collection of students' short stories about the war in Iraq.   As expected, several were accepted for publication in national magazines.

Please describe the applicant's greatest accomplishment.

Elizabeth demonstrated her impressive skills as a researcher while completing her senior class paper, "Women in British Literature."   As part of her research, Elizabeth took the initiative to locate and interview several direct descendants of Jane Austen, who provided invaluable insight into the author's motivation and perspective.   Elizabeth Reed, the great-grandniece of Ms. Austen, graciously provided Elizabeth with Jane's original notes for "Pride and Prejudice," which had never been made available to the public.   Elizabeth's paper included a rich discussion of Ms. Austen's private thoughts on several notable historical events, which are eloquently captured in her writing.   After reading Elizabeth's paper, I had a greater understanding of life in Ms. Austen's time and the challenges she faced as an author.   I subsequently re-read "Pride and Prejudice" with a more enlightened perspective.   Thanks to Elizabeth's herculean efforts, her paper was a magnificent example of narrative and descriptive writing.

In what area does the applicant need improvement?

Elizabeth currently negotiates her own deals with the magazines and publishing companies that buy her work.   With a business education, she will be better prepared to understand and negotiate the contracts they present her.

Is there anything else we should know about the applicant?

Overall, Elizabeth is a talented, conscientious and dedicated woman.   I am certain that she has the abilities and drive to accomplish whatever she sets her mind to.   She will inevitably succeed in the business side of publishing.

Our Assessment: This letter provides a short and well-documented discussion of Elizabeth's achievements as a writer.   She is clearly a woman who is willing to use her skills on behalf of interests and causes that are significant to her.   The committee was impressed not only by Elizabeth's many publications, but by her kind heart and charitable nature.   Her background in publishing was a great fit for the business school that she eventually chose.

Letter #6:   From Professor

How long have you known the applicant and in what capacity?

Please accept this letter of support for Lucas Gardner's application for business school.   Lucas is a 2008 graduate of the University of Texas at Austin, where I am an Associate Professor of Psychology.   In his four years with us, he completed four of my classes, including Social & Developmental Psychology and the Psychology of Addictions. He was an exceptional student: intelligent, enthusiastic and assertive.   Lucas's perceptive comments, peppered with his wry sense of humor, invariably brought our classroom discussions to a higher level.   From my observation, Lucas's writing and reasoning skills were comparable to those of the doctoral candidates in our department.   He has a bright future in academic research, if he chooses to pursue it.

What is the applicant's greatest strength?   Please give an example.

In addition to his considerable academic strengths, Lucas is a gifted and prolific researcher.   As a junior, he enrolled in Psycho-Biological Research Methodology, a graduate-level course which required students to complete an entire research project (from literature review to final paper) in just one semester.   Lucas tackled his project with gusto and completed his paper in time to present his results at the annual American Psychological Research Symposium (APRS) in St. Louis.   Without a doubt, Lucas's presentation was one of the best at the conference.   He demonstrated remarkable composure, particularly during the grueling question-and-answer session, in which he was besieged with inquiries that went beyond the scope of his work.   I was impressed by Lucas's ability to think on his feet under such stressful circumstances.

Please describe the applicant's greatest accomplishment.

During his senior year, Lucas completed a follow-up project to address the questions he had been asked at the previous APRS conference.   His subsequent presentation at the annual meeting won first place in the undergraduate research competition.   To my delight, Lucas has already begun to build a professional network at these conferences by chatting with peers from other institutions about their research.   His intellectual curiosity is unparalleled for someone his age.

In his latest project, Lucas developed a novel questionnaire for use in surveys with grade school participants.   Unlike traditional forms, which require a fourth-grade literacy level, Lucas's form uses a clever combination of symbols and scales to solicit data from younger subjects.   Upon its presentation at the 2008 APRS, the questionnaire caught the eye of Dr. Charles Raines, the President and CEO of Omega Marketing, Inc.   Seeing its potential for use in evaluating children's products, Lucas patented the form and is currently negotiating a licensing agreement with Dr. Raines' firm.   As you might expect, Lucas's success in developing and marketing a product for consumer use has been an exciting and inspirational experience for our entire department.   We are quite proud of what he has been able to achieve in such a short period of time.

In what area does the applicant need improvement?

During his first two years on campus, Lucas was painfully shy, which prevented him from participating in many outside activities. Thankfully, in his junior year, Lucas made a concerted effort to conquer his shyness and make new friends.   By the time he began his research project, Lucas was comfortable enough in his own skin to give oral presentations in front of a large group of people.   As part of his MBA program, I am confident that he will continue to hone this skill.

Is there anything else we should know about the applicant?

As his advisor, I have been most impressed by Lucas's strong sense of moral responsibility.   When the University of Texas implemented an Honor Code in 2007, Lucas was one of its strongest supporters.   In class, Lucas eloquently explained how the Honor Code would enhance the reputation of all Texas graduates, because it would assure future employers that a candidate's grades were earned honestly.   I respected Lucas's willingness to follow his heart and support an unpopular position.   I am certain that he will bring the same strong sense of honor and integrity to business school.

Lucas's success is attributable to his rare combination of intelligence, motivation, communication skills and personal strengths.   He is an extremely well-balanced young man with the ability to form strong positive relationships with his peers and faculty members.   In his leisure time, Lucas served as a volunteer in the campus recruiting office and helped with a number of community fund-raising projects.   As expected, he brought a strong sense of enthusiasm and goodwill to all of these endeavors.

I recommend Lucas without hesitation, as he is an outstanding young man in every sense of the word.   You will enjoy having him as a student.

Our Assessment: This letter provides an extensive, well-documented discussion of Lucas's strengths as a student, researcher and campus leader.   In several places, the author explains how the candidate's skills will be useful in business school.   From an admissions perspective, the most compelling section of the letter is the paragraph about integrity; Lucas's ability and willingness to stand up for his principles impressed every member of the admissions committee.   By taking the time to document these exemplary personal strengths, which the committee would not otherwise have known about, this professor gave Lucas's candidacy a tangible boost.

Chapter 7:   Letters from Employers / Supervisors

In addition to a letter from a faculty member, business schools will also expect a letter from a candidate's employer (or supervisor).   For older candidates who are working full-time, this letter should document your professional achievements since you graduated from college, which can give you an edge over more recent graduates.   Ideally, the letter should be written by your direct supervisor (or another person in your chain of command).

If you cannot provide a letter from your boss without jeopardizing your job, you should submit a letter from a client or peer, rather than a supervisor.   But you MUST send a letter from someone who can document your performance in your most recent position.   As we discussed in Chapter 2, the "ideal" person to write your letter is someone who:

a.   understands the intellectual demands of business school
b.   knows you well enough to evaluate your qualifications
c.   is willing/able to provide enough supporting detail to justify his/her assessment

Letters from supervisors should include the following information:

a.   the type and extent of your professional experiences
b.   your career progression thus far, including any awards or promotions
c.   the specific skills you use in your position (and how they relate to a business career)
d.   your personality and stamina

In Paragraph 1, the author should explain his/her relationship with you, including:

His/her title and employer
How long (s)he has known you
Your relationship to him/her
The nature (and extent) of your professional interactions

In paragraph 2 (and possibly 3):   the author should briefly state his/her overall impression of you as a candidate. Then, (s)he should mention the specific qualities that you have demonstrated in your interactions with him/her. Remember, for business school recommendation letters, the power is in the details.   Do not simply list the candidate's job duties. Instead, take the time to document the *specific talents or skills* the person has demonstrated in that position.

Obviously, a candidate's accomplishments will depend upon his/her education and job title.   No two applicants will be exactly alike, which means that there is no "right" or "wrong" information for an author to include.   Our best advice is to describe the person's accountabilities and how well (s)he has fulfilled them.   But don't simply offer a laundry list of responsibilities; instead, you should focus on *one or two exceptional traits* that you have personally observed the candidate demonstrate in your interactions with him/her.

Ideally, the letter will also include specific examples to support the praise.   For example, if a letter claims that a candidate is a good writer, the author must mention a specific paper or assignment that the candidate completed in an extraordinary way.   What was the topic? The length?   What was terrific about the paper – was it short, concise, well documented, or unusually insightful?   Be specific.

In the next paragraph: All candidates, regardless of their background or profession, are expected to demonstrate the general character traits that business schools value, which are listed on the rating scale.   They include:

1.   Intellectual curiosity, common sense
2.   Motivation, reliability, perseverance
3.   Judgment, resourcefulness, communication skills
4.   Interpersonal skills, emotional stability, self-confidence, empathy, maturity

Authors should document these points in the following paragraph, by mentioning the candidate's habits and relationships at work.   Is (s)he motivated, resourceful, and reliable?   Does (s)he require a lot of direction or very little?   Does (s)he coast by or constantly look for new ways to contribute?   Document it in the letter.   If possible, the author should also document the candidate's ability to work in a team environment.   Is (s)he a natural leader?   Did (s)he pull his/her weight on any team projects or presentations?   If so, offer specific details.

In the penultimate paragraph: mention any other notable facts about the candidate that you want to convey. This section of the letter has the most flexibility, depending upon the candidate's background and what you have personally observed. Good points to include:

a. Participation in outside activities that relate to the candidate's job (or a business career)
b. Entrepreneurial ventures the candidate has launched
c. The ability to succeed in the face of adversity. As we discussed in Chapter 5, this can be tricky if the candidate does not want you to reveal the information. Nevertheless, there are situations in which the committee cannot properly assess the candidate's character and motivation unless they know the whole story.

From our perspective, the following factors are worth mentioning:

a. The candidate was a top performer, despite wrestling with serious personal challenges at home (divorce, death, familial illness, language or cultural barriers).
b. The candidate faced a daunting challenge in his/her job, but handled it in a mature and inspirational way.

Although these issues are private – and deeply difficult to talk about – the way a candidate deals with them is an indication of his/her maturity and character. If you have the applicant's permission to mention the issue – and you are willing to do so – you can provide the committee with insight into the candidate's life that they never could have acquired any other way.

In the final paragraph: put your opinion of the candidate into the proper perspective. How many people have you supervised at the candidate's level? How does the candidate compare to that group – the top 1%, 5%, or 20%? If you have specific experience with candidates who have obtained an MBA, it is particularly helpful to compare the candidate to that group. If the applicant is equally intelligent, motivated, and dynamic, this is the place to mention it.

In the closing statement: offer a brief summary of the candidate's qualifications and state the strength of your recommendation (enthusiastic, without reservation, etc.). In the last sentence, you should provide your contact information (phone number and email address) in case the committee wants to confirm your letter or acquire additional details. Although it is highly unlikely that someone will contact you, your letter will have an added level of credibility if you indicate that you are accessible to the reader.

Finally, print your letter on your official letterhead and sign it as follows:

John Smith, J.D.	Name, Academic Degree
Attorney	Formal Title
Smith & Wesson Law Firm	Affiliation

Here are several recommendation letters for business school candidates that were written by their supervisors. To protect the privacy of the writer and applicant, the names of all people, classes, schools, places, and companies have been changed.

Letter #7: Manager

I first met Lincoln Scott in September of 2006, when I hired him to work for me as a Marketing Research Analyst at Entertainment Solutions, which is a full-service research firm for music and entertainment companies. Our primary responsibilities are to monitor consumer trends and behavior in the industry and to make proactive recommendations to our clients based upon them. Since joining the firm, Lincoln has helped us to find more efficient, cost-effective means of gathering and analyzing our respondent data.

In 2007, Lincoln managed our largest – and most high profile – project to identify the core audience (and projected advertising revenue) for HBO's proposed children's network. To achieve this goal, he created a computer-based survey questionnaire, monitored the data collection process, and analyzed the survey results. By using a creative approach, Lincoln quickly re-defined our expectations of a good project manager. He discussed our needs with senior managers at HBO and drafted an interview script that was short, efficient, and precise. Then, Lincoln worked odd hours to monitor the interviewers as they began to field this 10,000-person study. After observing them for a few days, Lincoln streamlined the script by removing redundancies and improving the flow for the interviewers. For his creative and efficient approach, he received high praise from both the interviewers and the director of our phone center.

Lincoln also made several highly constructive suggestions to improve our interviewing process. On his own initiative, he wrote a memo to key managers that suggested a simple change in methodology that reduced our costs by $300,000. He also suggested alternative wordings for several interview questions that were unintentionally ambiguous. Lincoln's recommendations were well received by senior managers at both Entertainment Solutions and HBO, both for their value to the project and the sensitive way he presented them. Our contact at HBO was sufficiently impressed that he requested Lincoln's participation on all future studies.

To process the survey results, Lincoln used several advanced statistical techniques, including Cluster Analysis and Discriminant Analysis. He further demonstrated his analytical abilities by creating a new model for us to use when we bid on new accounts. In 2008, Lincoln helped us to customize a canned statistical program to analyze our data, which generated an additional $500,000 in annual cost savings. I have rarely seen another employee make such significant contributions to our firm.

Lincoln is an exceptional speaker with an impressive command of English, Spanish and Portuguese. He has also perfected his writing skills over the past few years. In client meetings, his attentive listening and great enthusiasm has helped him to propose and implement creative solutions to tough problems. Lincoln's amiable personality is also a strong asset; he is confident yet self-deprecating, with a dry sense of humor. As a result, Lincoln quickly formed solid relationships with subordinates, peers, clients and members of our management team. Managers in other departments frequently seek his advice, particularly for important company initiatives.

In every area of evaluation, Lincoln Scott has exceeded my highest expectations and has outshined others in his peer-group at Entertainment Solutions. His efforts were recently rewarded with a promotion to the position of Senior Research Analyst, which normally requires 10 years of professional experience. Based on Lincoln's solid performance, I am confident that he will be a serious and enthusiastic student at your school. I offer him my strongest recommendation.

Our Assessment: This letter provided a comprehensive review of Lincoln's achievements in a highly challenging position. By doing so, the author augmented the material in Lincoln's essays and confirmed his skills in business, languages, and statistics. The committee was favorably impressed.

Letter #8: From Supervisor

I am happy to recommend Patrick Wynn for admission to XXXX Business School.   Patrick worked under my direct supervision as a Graphic Artist and Designer for a five-year period at Zenith Advertising, which handles the marketing and advertising needs for several international consumer product companies.   Overall, he was an excellent employee who fulfilled the duties of his position in an exemplary way.

As an artist and designer, Patrick consistently produced high quality work in a timely fashion.   When asked, he always came up with ideas for our clients that were innovative and fresh.   Patrick's first project was the advertising campaign for Geisha Tuna, which was a $12 million dollar account.   By the time the Geisha team approached us, they had already screened and rejected most of our competitors.   Landing their business was a long shot, but we accomplished it, thanks mostly to Patrick.   After researching their target market, he came up with a creative concept for their television and print ads that touted the health benefits of tuna for women and children.   This resonated strongly with the Geisha CEO, who was looking for a way to capture the juvenile market.   At their insistence, Patrick became the point person for the account and handled all of their creative issues.   The feedback we received about Patrick was overwhelmingly positive.

Patrick also produced great work on the technical side of the business.   On his own initiative, Patrick completed a web design class and quickly became our in-house expert at Dreamweaver and Flash animation.   Whenever possible, he used the technology in our ad campaigns and on our newly redesigned website.   Patrick's most recent achievement was adding a digitized video stream to the web site, which allows us to showcase our most promising ad concepts to prospective clients without incurring the travel costs of traditional sales calls.   In the ten months it has been on the site, the video stream has attracted nearly 300,000 hits and has generated dozens of inquiries for our services.   In late 2007, we were named the Most Creative Site by the American Advertising Council, out of more than 200 sites on the internet.   We couldn't be more pleased by this positive response.

During his tenure with us, Patrick matured into an excellent manager.   When he assumed responsibility for the Geisha account, he became a supervisor for the first time, which required him to coordinate the work of two junior artists and a technician.   At first, Patrick seemed overwhelmed by the responsibility and was tempted to micromanage his people.   Fortunately, early on, he took the initiative to have several constructive discussions with his team members about expectations and communication.   They quickly learned to work together; afterwards, they delivered all projects within their time and budget restrictions.

Patrick recently left the firm when his wife accepted a faculty position at the University of Pennsylvania.   We discussed his interest in obtaining an MBA at the time of his departure.   Knowing Patrick as well as I do, I think it is an excellent decision for him.   He is a hard working man, analytical by nature, who communicates well with others.   He is loyal to a fault and not afraid to champion a worthy cause or to resolve a professional disagreement.   In all situations, he handles himself with grace and good humor.   You will enjoy having him as a student.

I have no hesitation in recommending Patrick Wynn for your program.   Should you require further elaboration, don't hesitate to contact me at 555-555-5555.

Our Assessment: This letter not only sells the candidate's technical and administrative strengths, but puts a positive spin on his early difficulties as a manager.   By citing Patrick's ability to negotiate with his team and build a productive relationship with them, the author highlights his maturity and judgment.   His comments were well-perceived.

Letter #9: From Employer / Supervisor

I have known Zoe Davis since 1997, when she joined the advertising department of *Women's Fitness* magazine. In 2005, Zoe moved to our Chicago office on a special assignment to establish our company's Internet presence. When Zoe returned to head office in 2008, she became my employee, since I had been promoted to Vice President of Advertising Operations the previous year.

From her first days at the magazine, Zoe demonstrated an amazing flair for sales and advertising. At the time, *Women's Fitness* had never tried to permeate the markets outside Canada and the United States. Zoe's charge was to sell advertising for an eclectic group of corporate clients in Europe, Asia and South America who were unfamiliar with our publication. Despite her young age, Zoe performed her primary role in an efficient and professional manner. Utilizing her command of French, Spanish and German, she forged several successful relationships with our European advertisers and distributors, who helped her to make additional business contacts. In just three years, *Women's Fitness* achieved a 40% market share in Europe, which exceeded our expectations. Even in Asia, where women rarely conducted business transactions, Zoe made significant inroads with key advertisers.

Zoe also excelled at the quantitative aspects of the job, which required her to gather and analyze data from diverse parties and make complex financial projections. Zoe's analyses were subsequently used to select the lowest cost vendors. In this capacity, she demonstrated that she was a quick learner and an excellent multi-tasker. I was particularly impressed by how quickly and seamlessly Zoe was able to provide support to the Accounting Group during our annual audits, which required her to learn how to process complex financial transactions.

After five years as an advertising assistant, Zoe was promoted to copywriter in 2002, a position that she held for nearly three years. As an advertising copywriter and direct marketing expert, she is among the best in the business. Zoe has a gift for writing, and her creative mind was responsible for some of the most successful marketing campaigns that *Women's Fitness* has ever implemented. In 2004, Zoe was hand-picked by senior management to work in Atlanta with the Internet Project Team. As team leader, she led the group responsible for adapting our direct mail campaigns to the Internet. The company implemented the team's strategy in early 2006, making *Women's Fitness* one of the top three publishers on the Web.

During the 2008 recession, our company endured a major downsizing event, which reduced our total headcount from 1200 to 180. Zoe was one of the few people to survive the layoffs, because she was simply too valuable to let go. When her group disbanded, Zoe stayed on as a manager in our training department. With her strong background in languages, Zoe was uniquely qualified to train new employees to implement the company's mailing campaigns across the globe. She has been highly successful in this capacity, increasing our subscription revenues in Asia by 69% in just one fiscal year. Thanks to Zoe, *Women's Fitness* has established a solid presence in Asian markets that were formerly considered impenetrable.

On an interpersonal basis, Zoe is truly a pleasure to work with. She displays a friendly, helpful and outgoing demeanor at all times. Consequently, she is well-liked by both her colleagues and managers. In hindsight, I am certain that Zoe's rapport with our multicultural clientele has generated significant revenue for us. She has an intuitive understanding of the service aspect of our business.

In closing, as I hope the above clearly attests, I think that Zoe Davis is an exceptionally bright and hardworking individual who throws herself enthusiastically into whatever she undertakes. Accordingly, I have no hesitation whatsoever in recommending Zoe for admission to business school.

Our Assessment: The strength of this letter is that it documents Zoe's impressive track record of career advancement in a declining industry. It also provides specific examples of strengths that are highly prized in the admissions process. Even small details, such as Zoe's background in foreign languages, enhanced the committee's positive opinion of her.

Letter #10:   From Supervisor

For the past six years, Jill Miller has been the Administrative Manager at the Health First Rehabilitative Center, where I am the Vice President of Operations.   During this time, she has become an expert in the numerous federal, state and local laws that govern all aspects of hospital administration.

Jill's first major achievement was putting a system in place to ensure that we passed our certification inspection.   At first, I feared that we would need to hire an expensive consultant to organize our files and manuals. To my surprise, Jill told me that it wouldn't be necessary, because she had already compiled and edited much of the material.   Long before our deadline, Jill had reviewed all of our protocols for our nurses, therapists and aides.   As a result, she was well aware of what we needed to do to pass the inspection.   By collecting and organizing the information from the right sources, including various government agencies, Jill created new documents that met the rigid (and sometimes conflicting) local, state, and federal guidelines.   As a result, we passed our initial inspection without the assistance of a specialized consultant.

To acknowledge her exemplary performance, I promoted Jill to the position of Administrative Manager in June of 2006.   In this capacity, she provides guidance and support on all managerial issues for our 120-bed, 230-employee facility, which enjoys an enviable 95% occupancy rate.   Without exception, Jill is an innovative self-starter who rarely needs supervision.   Her greatest skill is flexibility – regardless of how busy she is, Jill will do whatever is necessary to get the job done.   By becoming an expert at all aspects of our business, including hiring, training, customer service, and innumerable regulatory issues, Jill has been indispensable to our success.

Jill is an excellent communicator who gets along with all different types of people.   While training our employees, she shows an admirable level of patience and an uncanny attention to detail.   Jill is also the "go to" person in our office.   Whenever anyone has a question about a particular patient, family, or situation, they immediately ask her for help.   If Jill does not have the answer, she will make it her business to find it.

By living and working overseas, Jill also brings a level of cultural sensitivity to her professional interactions. She is fluent in Spanish and Portuguese, which enables her to converse with people who speak those languages. On several occasions, Jill has translated documents for patients and employees who needed her assistance.   As expected, she handled each request with the highest level of respect and confidentiality.

Jill has also impressed me with the high quality of her writing, both in her daily correspondence and in the policy and procedure manuals that she has written.   In compiling the material, Jill presented complex legal and medical terminology in a clear and concise way.   Every quarter, Jill updates all of our protocols to incorporate any changes in government regulations.   By doing so, she has established a good working relationship with the many agencies that govern our industry, including the inspectors who review our written documentation.

In the past six years, Jill has performed all of her responsibilities in an exemplary manner.   From my perspective, her only weakness is her tendency to be hard on herself, because she sets extremely high standards for her own performance.   Thankfully, Jill also finds great joy in her work, which makes her a positive role model for everyone at Health First.

In my long career in health care administration, no one has impressed me as positively as Jill Miller.   In her six years at Health First, Jill has been an innovative self-starter who has improved the efficiency of our business and earned the respect of her clients and peers.   She will be a valuable asset to whatever MBA program she joins.

<u>Our Assessment</u>:   This is a wonderful recommendation for a young woman who put herself through college while working full-time at Health First.   After reading about Jill's achievements at in a highly demanding job, the committee knew that she possessed the maturity and initiative to handle a rigorous MBA program.

Letter #11:   From Supervisor (Sales)

How long have you known the applicant and in what capacity?

For the past five years, Rose Landman has worked as the National Sales Director for Liberty Medical Supply.   In this role, she has created and maintained our sales in the lower 48 states and represented our firm at several North American trade shows. She has also supervised the work of eight Regional Sales Managers, who are located in different cities.   By supervising Rose during this period, I have gained a realistic assessment of the many skills she will bring to business school.

What is the applicant's greatest strength?   Please give an example.

When Rose came onboard, Liberty had eight regional sales offices with no national manager – as a result, they tended to work independently.   Rose faced several challenges to coordinate the work of her sales people, who were scattered in different locations across the United States.   Thankfully, she is a highly organized woman with extraordinary analytical skills.   During her first weeks on the job, Rose reviewed our records to identify ways we could gain additional business from our existing accounts.   She also assessed the needs and trends in the industry –from a technical, manufacturing, and business standpoint – to solve problems and identify new sales opportunities.

Rose exhibited superior skills in this area, which is critical in our business.   She identified many new sales leads in unexplored areas, such as military and veteran's hospitals, which were highly profitable for Liberty.   Rose's dynamic personality was a considerable asset to her in this process - she was gracious enough to work effectively with an eclectic group of people to negotiate the military contracts.   At the same time, she was tenacious enough to gather the voluminous documentation that these government accounts required.

Please describe the applicant's greatest accomplishment.

Thanks to Rose, we enjoyed 65% annual sales growth between 2004 and 2008, mostly due to the lucrative new accounts that she landed.   Her performance, on both a qualitative and quantitative basis, consistently exceeded my expectations.   In my career, I have rarely met anyone as disciplined and motivated as Rose.   Although she had no prior experience in the medical industry, she quickly brought herself up to speed on our needs and expectations. She also earned our certification as an official government vendor, which was extremely difficult to do.   During her five years at Liberty, Rose has proven to be equally successful at procuring new business and maintaining and growing our existing accounts. Our feedback from customers, including some of the top CEOs in the health care industry, has been exemplary.

On a personal level, Rose has also grown into a competent and effective manager.   When she first joined our team, Rose faced a difficult challenge: to supervise people in a field in which she had little or no experience.   From the start, Rose took the time to establish a solid rapport with her Regional Sales Managers, who had already built successful relationships with our biggest clients.   After earning their trust and support, she quickly got up to speed on our greatest opportunities and challenges.   I attribute Rose's smooth transition at least partially to the mature and respectful way that she treated her colleagues.

Rose is also one of the most effective sales people I have ever known.   When she visits a prospective client, she is literally prepared for anything – she has conducted her research, assessed the competition, and developed a winning sales proposition for the client.   Then, when she delivers her pitch, Rose calmly and methodically eliminates any objection the prospect may have about doing business with us.   As a result, Rose has an impressive record for closing deals in a highly competitive industry.   These skills will undoubtedly serve her well in her future career.

In what area does the applicant need improvement?

When she first came onboard, Rose's command of technology left something to be desired.   As a result, she occasionally wasted time trying to communicate via phone and snail mail with prospects that were only reachable via wireless technology.   When I suggested that Rose become more proficient in this area, she readily agreed.   Rose now communicates effectively with her team mates and customers using a laptop and BlackBerry.   She also became a huge proponent of virtual meetings and sales calls, which save us considerable money.   As part of her business degree, Rose will benefit from classes in computer science, which will keep her abreast of the changes in technologies that our business relies upon.   Otherwise, she will undoubtedly rely on the tried-and-true methods with which she is most comfortable.

Is there anything else we should know about the applicant?

Looking ahead, I am certain that Rose has what it takes to succeed in a competitive MBA program. Throughout her career, she has conquered many obstacles, including the prejudice against women in a male dominated industry. Most impressively, Rose has done so with an uncommon level of grace and integrity. If given the chance, she will be an excellent addition to your class.

Please contact me at XXX-XXX-XXXX or at email address if you require additional information.

Our Assessment: This letter, which was written by the CEO of a top medical supply company, verified the candidate's extraordinary sales skills, which were not articulated anywhere else in her application.   The letter also confirmed Rose's initiative in pursuing military accounts and her ability to close deals that require considerable documentation and flexibility.   Without this letter, the committee might not have seen Rose as the aggressive self-starter that she is.

Letter #12:   From Manager: Documents the Candidate's Strong Administrative Skills

How long have you known the applicant and in what capacity?

I have worked with Terrence Smith for over five years at Allied National Software, where I am the President and CEO. After serving as our creative manager during the company's startup, Terrence rapidly assumed responsibility for all aspects of systems administration.   Thanks to his diligence and creativity, we have enjoyed continual expansion and revenue growth ($4.5 million to $10 million in just five years).

What is the applicant's greatest accomplishment?

Terrence's greatest accomplishment is the database that he created to streamline and centralize communication and production within the company.   Terrence rallied for the change throughout his first two years with the firm and ultimately took the initiative to develop the system himself.   I was amazed by its effectiveness and ease of use. Terrence's custom database solution eliminates the paperwork and communication issues that plague most software firms.   It has literally revolutionized the way we do business.   What was most impressive was Terrence's initiative and motivation.   He completed the project on his own time, with no prodding from senior management and no guarantee of success.   His goal was not self-promotion, but to improve the way the company functions.

Analytical by nature, Terrence is a fast learner with an impressive command of software technology.   He troubleshoots complicated situations with ease, simultaneously computing multiple scenarios to identify the optimal solution.   To a lay person, it seems like Terrence simply "knows" the answer, when he is actually applying years of training and skill to each situation.   Even under stressful circumstances, he has an amazing ability to remember and apply standards and technical rules.

Based on your experience with this applicant, please describe his/her level of enthusiasm/energy. Please provide some examples.

When Terrence first approached me about the job, he said he was willing to do "whatever it took" to prove his worth. Since then, he has far exceeded my expectations, both through the volume of his work and the conscientiousness he has brought to the firm.   Under Terrence's direction, Allied National Software has survived the rapid consolidation and outsourcing in the technology industry.   Terrence created his department from the ground up, setting the standards for our software and handling all aspects of troubleshooting and quality control.   Terrence has also taken the initiative to update our computer network and databases.   By working "in the trenches" with our manufacturing team in China, he has set an amazing example of efficiency and productivity.

Please assess this candidate's ability to work effectively in teams.

Terrence's responsibilities require a rare combination of technical, administrative and interpersonal strengths. Fortunately, he handles all of these challenges with confidence.   Terrence is a quintessential "team player;" in leadership situations, he is the glue that holds the team together, creating a healthy environment for a creative exchange of ideas.   Whenever possible, he offers guidance and training to subordinates who want to learn more. By employing these strengths, Terrence's work teams are highly successful and often surpass our clients' expectations.

Terrence communicates well will all types of people, including those with non-technical backgrounds.   Terrence routinely prepares and delivers project presentations to clients and senior managers.   He has an excellent command of English and a polished presentation style.   On a personal level, Terrence has a congenial personality and a great sense of humor.   He is honest to a fault and highly supportive of those around him.

In what areas does the applicant need the most improvement?

Terrence's chief drawback is his tendency to be a perfectionist and expect too much from himself.   During his first years with the firm, he resisted delegating because he was afraid that his employees would not complete the tasks correctly.   Fortunately, Terrence has learned to better pace himself and manage his time.   By doing so, he has increased the quality and quantity of work that he can deliver.   Not surprisingly, he has also become a more nurturing manager who allows his people to shine

Additional Comments :

As his boss, I have bittersweet feelings about Terrence's decision to pursue his MBA. Although we are poised for continual growth, my company cannot offer Terrence the professional challenges that he richly deserves. My loss will be your program's gain. If you would like additional details about Terrence, please feel free to contact me at 555-555-5555. I offer him my full support.

<u>Our Assessment</u>: This letter provides an excellent personal and professional endorsement for a seasoned technical manager. Although the author could not state *why* the candidate wanted to go to business school, he convinced the reader that Terrence was certainly up to the task. Fortunately, one of Terrence's other recommendations explained his long-term goals, including his longstanding interest in working for a non-profit group. As a result, the committee was better able to understand Terrence's motivation for making a career change at this point in time.

Chapter 8:   Letters from Co-Workers, Clients & Peers

In some cases, it is impossible for candidates to provide a letter of recommendation from their current employer without risking their job.   The moment their supervisor knows that they are planning to leave their position to go to business school, their future at the firm is in jeopardy.   Nevertheless, it is imperative for candidates who are working full-time to provide a letter of recommendation from someone who can document their performance in their current position.   Otherwise, it is difficult for the committee to assess the maturity and professional skills the candidate will bring to the table.

If it is impossible to get a reference from someone in your own chain of command, you should submit a letter from a co-worker, client or peer who can provide an objective assessment of your performance.   As we discussed in Chapter 2, the "ideal" person to write your letter is someone who:

a.   understands the intellectual demands of business school
b.   knows you well enough to evaluate your qualifications
c.   is willing/able to provide enough supporting detail to justify his/her assessment

Letters from co-workers or peers should include the following information:

a.   the type and extent of your professional experiences
b.   your career progression thus far, including any awards or promotions
c.   the specific skills you use in your position (and how they relate to a business career)
d.   your personality and stamina

In Paragraph 1, the author should explain his/her relationship with you, including:

His/her title and employer
How long (s)he has known you
Your relationship to him/her
The nature (and extent) of your professional interactions

In paragraph 2 (and possibly 3):, the author should briefly state the *specific talents and skills* the candidate has demonstrated in his/her professional interactions.   Ideally, the letter will also include specific examples to support the praise.   For example, if a letter claims that a candidate is a good writer, the author must mention a specific paper or assignment that the candidate completed in an extraordinary way.   What was the topic? The length?   What was terrific about the paper – was it short, concise, well documented, or unusually insightful?   Be specific.

In the next paragraph:. All candidates, regardless of their background or profession, are expected to demonstrate the general character traits that business schools value, which are listed on the rating scale.   They include:

1.   Intellectual curiosity, common sense
2.   Motivation, reliability, perseverance
3.   Judgment, resourcefulness, communication skills
4.   Interpersonal skills, emotional stability, self-confidence, empathy, maturity

Authors should document these points by discussing the candidate's habits and relationships at work.   Is (s)he motivated, resourceful, and reliable?   Does (s)he coast by or constantly look for new ways to contribute?   Document it in the letter.   If possible, the author should also document the candidate's ability to work in a team environment.   Is (s)he a natural leader?   Did (s)he pull his/her weight on any team projects or presentations?   If so, offer specific details.

In the penultimate paragraph: mention any other notable facts about the candidate that you want to convey.

This section of the letter has the most flexibility, depending upon the candidate's background and what you have personally observed.   Good points to include:

a.   Participation in outside activities related the candidate's job (or a business career)
b.   Entrepreneurial ventures the candidate has launched
c.   The ability to succeed in the face of adversity.   As we discussed in Chapter 5, this can be tricky if the candidate does not want you to reveal the information.   Nevertheless, there are situations in which the committee cannot

properly assess the candidate's character and motivation unless they know the whole story.

From our perspective, the following factors are worth mentioning:

a. The candidate was a top performer, despite wrestling with serious personal challenges at home (divorce, death, familial illness, language or cultural barriers).
b. The candidate faced a daunting challenge in his/her job, but handled it in a mature and inspirational way.

Although these issues are private – and deeply difficult to talk about – the way a candidate deals with them is an indication of his/her maturity and character. If you have the applicant's permission to mention the issue – and you are willing to do so – you can provide the committee with insight into the candidate's life that they never could have acquired any other way.

In the final paragraph: put your opinion of the candidate into the proper perspective. How many people have you worked with at the candidate's level? How does the candidate compare to that group – is (s)he in the top 1%, 5%, or 20%? If you have specific experience with candidates who have obtained an MBA, it is particularly helpful to compare the candidate to that group. If the applicant is equally intelligent, motivated, and dynamic, this is the place to mention it.

In the closing statement: offer a brief summary of the person's qualifications and state the strength of your recommendation (enthusiastic, without reservation, etc.). In the last sentence, you should provide your contact information (phone number and email address) in case the committee wants to confirm your letter or acquire additional details. Although it is highly unlikely that someone will contact you, your letter will have an added level of credibility if you make yourself accessible to the reader.

Finally, print your letter on your official letterhead and sign it as follows:

John Smith	Name
Marketing Manager	Formal Title
Kraft, Inc.	Affiliation

Here are several recommendation letters for business school candidates that were written by co-workers, clients and peers. To protect the privacy of the writer and applicant, the names of all people, classes, schools, places, and companies have been changed.

Letter #13: From a Peer in the Entertainment Industry

For the past three years, Dominique DuPres has worked with me as a graphic artist in the feature film division at Columbia Pictures. After observing her diligence, intelligence and solid work ethic, I recommend her without qualification for the Harvard MBA program.

While working on the three *Harry Potter* movies, Dominique and I frequently put together creative presentations that outlined our artistic approach to the project, including myriad illustrations and photographic reference materials. Dominique's creativity, resourcefulness and ability to see a project through to completion really made these presentations distinctive and successful.

When we went into production on the first Harry Potter movie, Dominique worked with people in all areas of production, from the ideation stage through the eventual release of the film. During this time, she was an effective communicator who served as the liaison with scattered members of the crew. Dominique also coordinated projects that required the cooperation of crew members on international location shoots, which revealed her outstanding ability to work collaboratively while guiding the project quickly and effectively.

In 2008, Dominique's leadership on a stressful shoot earned her a promotion to Senior Graphic Artist. At the very last moment, we discovered that we needed to re-conceive several action sequences that had already been storyboarded. It was after midnight and we had to refigure the scenes for an expensive 8 am shoot. Dominique quickly found a new storyboard artist and worked with him throughout the night on several potential drafts. At 5 am, she ran the most promising scenarios by the stunt coordinator and the cinematographer to make sure that the new sequences worked. Then, she communicated the new plans with crew members from all departments, making sure that everyone was up-to-date on the relevant changes. At 7 am, after a long, sleepless night, she even jumped in to draw a few last-minute storyboard changes herself. Thanks to Dominique's diligence, the director never knew about our last-minute emergency. He shot the scenes on schedule, without fanfare or overtime costs.

In an industry filled with big egos and impossible challenges, Dominique's sensitivity, diligence, and high energy level made working with her a joy. In fact, I am hard pressed to remember a situation in which I did not learn something from Dominique about how to do my job better. In the past three years, she has been an exceptional worker, role model and friend.

With her amazing creativity, Dominique has what it takes to advance to a position in which she will evaluate prospective properties and guide their creative vision. She has certainly paid her dues by mastering her skills as a writer, photographer, and editor. Following her MBA, Dominique will be well positioned to return to a major studio and pursue a position on a senior management track. I, for one, will be the first person to try to work for her!

Please let me know if you need any additional information.

Our Assessment: This author did an exceptional job of showcasing Dominique's accomplishments in an entry-level job. The anecdote about her overnight conception of the storyboards was particularly impressive. Although this author does not have an MBA, she clearly understands the benefit of one in the entertainment industry. Her paragraph on Dominique's goals was concise and insightful.

Letter #14: From a Co-Worker, Client, or Peer

I am honored to write a reference letter for Lily Gray. I have known Lily since January of 2006, when she came to work for me at the Abbott Forensics Laboratory, where I am the Manager of Operations. Over the past three years, Lily has fulfilled her duties in an excellent manner.

Lily began as a technician in the front office, where she accepted specimens from our clients for analysis. Then, she completed the formal training program to learn how to perform various serological, microbiological, and histological tests. Although most new employees require a month to complete the training and handle specimens without supervision, Lily mastered the job within two weeks. Through sheer motivation, Lily became the fastest and most reliable technician in the front office.

After Lily graduated from college, we were delighted to hire her on a full-time basis. Because of her success in other departments, we promoted her in October of 2007 to a management position in the laboratory, which handles a variety of physical, chemical and biological analyses. Lily was promoted to department manager, which required her to restructure one of our busiest and most critical departments. With this promotion, Lily assumed responsibility for three key functions (sample collection, analysis, and data entry) and twelve employees. Because of the high volume of work and our fast-paced schedule, the previous manager of the laboratory had left in frustration. Lily stepped into an extremely demanding situation, which forced her to develop her management skills.

As a matter of corporate policy, we guarantee our clients a turnaround time of three to five days for most analytical tests. At the time of her promotion, Lily's lab was six weeks behind schedule and unable to catch up. Not surprisingly, Lily's people were overworked and discouraged. Even more challenging, Lily found herself in the awkward position of supervising people who had previously been her peers. Fortunately, she had the maturity to handle these circumstances in an amiable manner.

Lily used a hands-on approach to get her department back on track. She organized teams to eliminate the backlog and to establish an effective schedule for future work. She held departmental meetings to hear everyone's concerns and to improve morale. With no money for raises or promotions, Lily used creative incentives like candy and snacks to reward her people for a job well done. More importantly, she implemented several procedures to prevent future backlogs and to ensure consistent customer service. Thanks to Lily's enhanced organizational and interpersonal skills, her department is a model of teamwork and efficiency.

On one occasion, Lily's computer expertise was a tremendous help to our IT Department. After taking over the department, Lily questioned whether the data sheet that the front office used could be stored on the computer, rather than written by hand. She worked with the IT department to develop the computerized template that we currently use. The benefits have been tremendous; in addition to saving time in the lab, the new system eliminated one front office position, which freed that employee for other tasks. In a three-month period, the new computerized system stimulated $150,000 in cost savings for Abbott.

Over the years, Lily has eagerly accepted every challenge that we presented to her. Because her group handles diverse assignments, Lily must constantly juggle rigid deadlines and multiple priorities. Fortunately, organization is one of her leading strengths. On any given day, Lily's group may handle hundreds of specimens from hospitals throughout the city. Even under stressful circumstances, Lily can be trusted to complete her work flawlessly and graciously. Her ability to manage so many diverse tasks has been an inspiration to her colleagues.

Lily is a bright and hardworking woman who approaches life's challenges with focus and enthusiasm. I am certain that she will bring the same level of determination to your program.

<u>Our Assessment</u>: This is a wonderful letter that captures Lily's strengths as a manager. For candidates like Lily, who have spent their entire careers with a single employer, it is critical to obtain a letter that documents the depth and breadth of their professional experience. By the time the reader finishes this letter, (s)he has a better appreciation of what Lily does and the skills that are required for her to accomplish it. The author brought Lily's skills to life in a way that no resume or job description could.

Letter #15:   From a Co-Worker, Client, or Peer

Please accept this letter of recommendation for my colleague at Lehman Brothers, Caroline Steinman.   I have known Caroline since our undergraduate days at Yale, where we were roommates and sorority sisters.   After our graduation in 2002, we both joined Lehman Brothers in Miami as management trainees.   We have subsequently worked together on many professional and community projects.

Caroline is by far the most gifted financial analyst at Lehman Brothers.   She has an impressive knowledge of finance and an uncanny ability to predict trends in the equity markets.   In the eight years we have worked in the Miami office, she has handled the volatile technology sector, including the Internet stocks.   For much of 2005 and 2006, Caroline was considered a "contrarian" analyst because she refused to endorse what she felt was an overvalued sector. While many analysts jumped on the technology bandwagon, Caroline wisely held back.   Time proved her correct, as the bubble subsequently burst and many "Nasdaq darlings" have failed to recover.

In evaluating a company, Caroline's mantra is always "watch the fundamentals."   She has built a successful career by knowing that what's important is not the sizzle of a firm (its advertising or buzz), but the steak (its management strength and P/E ratio).   Caroline's life is also based on solid "fundamentals."   She is a kind and honest person who has helped many junior analysts learn the ropes at Lehman Brothers.   In addition to her significant responsibilities as an analyst, Caroline is always happy to pitch in with orientation and training duties within the department.   Whenever a newcomer has a question or concern, Caroline is the person they seek.   I strongly suspect that our low rate of turnover is at least somewhat due to Caroline's heartfelt assistance.

Throughout our mutual tenure at Lehman Brothers, Caroline has also been a leader in several volunteer and community organizations.   In the summer of 2004, she formed a non-profit group called Disaster Awareness to educate the public about emergency disaster preparation.   Before she could even gather supplies, Caroline was faced with the unprecedented challenges of Hurricanes Frances and Jeanne, which hit the East Coast in September.

With little money and only a few volunteers, Caroline helped the community survive the storm.   She walked to the local television station to deliver on-air advisories about evacuation and safety; she also went door-to-door to help elderly residents move to nearby shelters.   Amazingly, Caroline also found a safe place to house over one-hundred abandoned pets.   After the storm had passed, Caroline organized volunteers to remove tree branches from roads and bridges.   She took a leadership role in all aspects of the recovery process.

Ironically, Caroline doesn't consider her actions to be particularly heroic.   In her mind, she was simply doing what she needed to do in a crisis.   To those of us who know her well, that's the most special thing about Caroline: she does what is right, without complaint or reservation.   She is a kindhearted person who remains calm in a crisis and devotes herself to helping others.   I would trust her not only with my career, but with my life.   She is THAT honorable a person.

Sadly, in my career as a financial analyst, I have worked with many people who lack most of Caroline's character strengths.   Ultimately, I believe that is what makes her special, not just to Lehman Brothers, but to any organization she joins. If the power of a school is in its students, then your program will be significantly stronger if you admit Caroline Steinman.   She is one in a million.

<u>Our Assessment</u>:   The strength of this letter is in the details.   Every point is supported by a concrete example that puts the observation into its proper context.   This letter also provides an eloquent discussion of Caroline's rare combination of analytical and interpersonal strengths.   The reader walks away overwhelmingly impressed by Caroline's generosity and integrity.

Letter #16: From a Corporate Executive (and Public Figure)

Please accept this letter of recommendation for Ms. Geneva Garrett, who I have known in a professional capacity for the last three years of my employment with the XYZ Corporation.

Although Ms. Garrett has not worked directly for me, I have observed her work on a variety of projects and can attest to the following:

1. Geneva is a very personable, professional and ethical person, with the highest respect for the team concept that I have tried to cultivate at XYZ.   In 2008, she led the team that re-opened our office in Sacramento.   Her peers and subordinates have consistently praised Geneva's autocratic management style, which gives them the flexibility they need to complete their work quickly and efficiently.

2. Geneva is highly task oriented, and has been instrumental in working on projects that have resulted in significant cost savings for the company.   During my association with the firm, this is where Geneva has consistently proven her value.   Examples include her pivotal role in the sale of the manufacturing division and her many cost optimization initiatives with our telecommunications vendors.

3. In Geneva's six-year tenure with XYZ, more than 4,200 employees have been laid off and the firm has filed for bankruptcy protection.   Only the best and the brightest have retained their jobs, due to their demonstrated value to the company.   Geneva's contributions have been immeasurable, hence, she has survived every cutback.

Geneva is experienced in the preparation of financial statements, budget projections, statistical reporting, project management and financial/business analysis.   She has a solid work ethic and has performed well in a self-directed capacity for the majority of her career.   Despite the legal and financial challenges that XYZ has faced, Geneva has met tight deadlines and delivered top quality work.   I particularly commend Geneva for working a full-time job while earning her college degree at night.   This is a daunting task that I know from personal experience is very difficult to do.   I give Geneva my highest recommendation and I wish her well in all of her educational and professional pursuits.

Our Assessment: The author of this letter is a well-known public figure who was hired to re-structure the XYZ Corporation during its bankruptcy proceedings.   His high praise of Geneva, along with examples of her achievements, gave the letter an added boost.   By citing her tangible contributions to XYZ's reorganization, the author showed that Geneva has the loyalty and stamina to weather tough times.

Nevertheless, we would be remiss if we did not point out this letter's obvious flaws.   It is short; it also does not offer specific details to support the examples.   In this respect, this letter would NOT have been sufficient if it had been the only one the candidate had submitted from the XYZ Corporation.   Thankfully, Geneva's supervisor provided a second letter that conveyed the essential details that the committee needed to see.

Letter #17: From a Co-Worker and Friend (Dual degree applicant in business and law)

How long have you known the applicant and in what capacity?

I have known Steven Jones since 1999, when he joined my fraternity at Brown University. Since then, we have continued to interact as industry peers.

What is the applicant's greatest accomplishment?

Even as a teenager, Steven had a strong entrepreneurial spirit. At Brown, he identified the need for low-cost printer ink on campus. In response, he established and ran a company from his dorm room called Ink Jet solutions, which sold refurbished ink cartridges to students and faculty members. On a practical basis, the venture gave him real-life experience in branding, marketing, and distributing a consumer product. On a personal basis, it greatly increased Steven's self-confidence.

Inspired by this success, Steven embarked on a new venture to fill a void in publishing. While perusing the bookstores, he could not find any books that were aimed at teenage entrepreneurs. On his own initiative, Steven decided to write and publish one himself. In 2001, he created a company called Novice Publishing to market a self-help book entitled *Entrepreneurial Teens: Starting a Business that Breaks all the Rules.* Steven managed all aspects of the venture, from writing the draft, compiling the financial advice, and selecting the paper, font, and title image. He also marketed the book on numerous college web sites, which was an effective technique that traditional publishers had ignored. By doing so, Steven enjoyed tremendous success. In subsequent years, his book has won numerous awards and become a cult classic in various entrepreneurial circles. As his friend, I was amazed by Steven's ability to pursue an opportunity that others could not see.

What are the applicant's salient strengths?

At Brown, Steven completed a double major in Information Technology and Business Administration, which were an excellent match for his analytical skills. After he graduated, he joined the sales and marketing division at Sun Microsystems and advanced to the level of Marketing Manager within five years. In this role, Steven develops and implements business-to-business marketing programs to fuel the company's ongoing growth. He also hires, trains, and manages his own technical sales team.

One of Steven's greatest strengths is his analytical nature, which allows him to predict the consequences of different alternatives. As a result, he is an excellent planner who handles problems proactively, rather than reactively. At Brown, Steven used this ability to determine the long-term future of Novice Publishing when a large publishing house offered to buy the rights to *Entrepreneurial Teen*. Although he was flattered by the offer, Steven was reluctant to surrender the rights to a title that offered unlimited spin-off possibilities. He also feared that the large publishing house would not market *Entrepreneurial Teen* in the most effective manner. After evaluating the pros and cons of both alternatives, Steven declined the offer and hired a consultant to help him publish the follow-up titles in-house. By doing so, he could maintain the quality of his product and keep his hand in the marketing channels.

Please assess this candidate's ability to work effectively in teams.

Steven is an excellent communicator who is fluent in English, Spanish, Portuguese, and French. In business and personal settings, he expresses his thoughts in a clear and persuasive manner. Steven is also a voracious reader with an impressive breadth of knowledge – he can speak intelligently on topics as diverse as history and economics to sports and pop culture. Thanks to these skills, Steven can work effectively with diverse groups of people.

In his career at Sun Microsystems, Steven has led several project teams that have created and marketed new technologies on an abbreviated timeframe. His rapid career advancement in a competitive industry, coupled with his solid reputation with his peers, is a powerful testament to his ability to build and lead strong project teams.

Please comment on the applicant's personal integrity.

Over the past ten years, I have watched Steven handle several situations with the highest personal integrity. On one occasion, he had to lay off six members of his sales team when Sun decided to sell the product line they represented. Steven delivered the news in a compassionate manner, which alleviated the employees' grief and shock; he also used his connections to help the sales people find new jobs.

Another time, Steven created several unpaid internships in his department, to allow minority teens in his community to obtain invaluable business experience. Throughout the summer, he also took the time to meet with the teens and mentor them on various aspects of business. Because of Steven's efforts, two of the teens learned about scholarships that would allow them to attend college. Another teen, who had considered dropping out of school, decided to explore his newfound interest in computer science classes. To me, these activities were an excellent example of Steven's kindness and generosity. He had nothing to gain from creating these internships or working with the kids who accepted them. He simply wanted to do his part to help them succeed.

In what areas does the applicant need the most improvement?

Steven's only weakness is his tendency to overanalyze situations, which is an extension of his highly analytical nature. In college, his desire to consider all perspectives and contingencies impeded his ability to make decisions. Thankfully, in recent years, Steven has learned how to adapt his approach to suit the situation, which allows him to well-reasoned decisions in an efficient manner.

Additional Comments :

By continually challenging himself in various aspects of business, Steven has developed several critical strengths that will enhance his future career. If given a chance, he will make an extraordinary contribution to the JD/MBA program. I offer him my strongest recommendation.

Our Assessment: People often wonder what a recommendation letter from a close friend would (or *should*) look like. This letter is an excellent example. The author, in addition to being a successful software manager, is also a long-time friend of the candidate, which he discloses in the first paragraph. The beauty of the letter is that it does not stop there – the author proceeds to explain Steven's many accomplishments over the years in a persuasive and eloquent way. As a result, the reader knows that the candidate is a unique and creative self-starter.

How long have you known the applicant and in what capacity?

As the Group Vice President of Marketing for the Godiva Corporation, I provide executive direction to a firm that distributes gourmet chocolates and confections in the European markets.   Since 1973, we have expanded our business into a leading distributorship of 50 prestigious international brands, including Godiva Gold, which is the only European chocolate that is sold in Saudi Arabia.   To achieve such aggressive growth, we have relied upon the talents of our highly motivated employees, such as Mr. Mario Wing.   I have known Mario since March of 2004, when he was promoted to Product Manager in our London office.   I have subsequently spoken to Mr. Wing several times at regional meetings and have observed his presentations and conferences.   He is unquestionably one of the brightest and most talented managers we have ever employed.

How do you assess the applicant's leadership potential?

Mario's promotion into management left him directly accountable for all aspects of several confectionary brands, include a newly launched line of gourmet truffles in Rome.   At the time, it had been over ten years since Godiva had tried to enter the Italian market.   Accordingly, Mario faced many challenges to assess the market potential and launch a new brand.   Thankfully, he proved to be fully capable of meeting the challenge.   Within a matter of months, the brand's sales in Italy had greatly eclipsed those in the other seven countries in which it is distributed.   For the first time in history, Italy was the best performer in our group, contributing over 38% of the brand's total sales.   I credit these impressive results exclusively to Mario's instincts and aggressiveness.

Succeeding in the highly competitive gourmet food market requires a rare combination of creativity, dedication and business acumen.   From my observation, Mario is gifted in all three areas.   By nature, he is a highly creative young man who has a flair for global trends in luxury goods.   Mario is also curious and diligent enough to research areas in which he is not familiar.   When faced with an obstacle, Mario will find a creative solution, rather than adjust his goal.   He constantly impresses his superiors by achieving goals that were supposedly "impossible" to attain.   Most importantly, by facing new challenges with optimism and enthusiasm, Mario has brought a much-needed boost in energy to our London office.   His exceptional performance has increased the standard of excellence for other Godiva employees.

Based on your experience with this applicant, please describe his/her level of enthusiasm/energy. Please provide some examples.

In September of 2005, I had the pleasure of working directly with Mario at our regional sales meeting in London.   As part of the activities, Mario made an energetic and imaginative presentation to the executives from Harrods Department Stores, which licenses several of our premium brands.   Each part of the presentation, including the promotional activities, graphics, and merchandizing, was tailored to emphasize Harrods high-end concept value.   Thanks to Mario's presentation, Harrods doubled its order and agreed to sponsor a lucrative holiday promotion with the Godiva brand.   We could not have accomplished this without Mario's commitment.

Please assess this candidate's ability to work effectively in teams.

Mario works well on project teams.   During the launch of our gourmet truffle line in Prague, Mario participated in brainstorming sessions to identify a solution to a transportation issue in Spain, which had damaged nearly a ton of liquid caramel.   Later, Mario used his persuasive skills to "sell" his solution to senior managers.   After observing him in action, there is no doubt in my mind that Mario will be well prepared for all class discussions, both as a listener and as an active participant.

In what areas does the applicant need the most improvement?

Although Mario does not have formal business training, he is experienced in the preparation of financial statements, budget projections and marketing analyses.   He is also honest, personable and fully committed to adding value to our corporation.   Mario's only weakness is his tendency to play down his accomplishments, which can initially appear to be a lack of confidence.   As I have gotten to know him, however, I have realized that Mario's humble nature is simply part of his gracious personality.

Additional Comments :

Mario is not only an effective and ambitious professional, but a well-rounded person with many interests outside the office. Whenever possible, he encourages others to join the fun. When several of our colleagues were in town from Montreal, Mario organized several volleyball games between our two groups. The outings were terrific ice-breaking exercises. On another occasion, Mario suggested that several co-workers join him at the health club. In addition to its obvious athletic benefits, the experience was great fun for everyone who participated.

I am currently accountable for 600 employees in 8 regional branches (London, Paris, Dublin, Rome, Geneva, Madrid, Amsterdam and Prague). Without a doubt, Mario Wing is one of our most talented and dynamic managers. I recommend him for your program with the highest enthusiasm. Please contact me if you require further details about Mario's tenure at Godiva. I can be reached at XXXXXX@host.com.

Our Assessment: In many cases, candidates are unable to get letters from their direct supervisors for a variety of political reasons. This letter, which was written by a VP in a completely different department, presented exactly the information the committee needed to see. As always, the strength of this letter is the extensive, well-documented discussion of Mario's strengths. By providing third-party verification of Mario's organizational, planning and interpersonal skills, the author highlighted many achievements that the committee would never have heard about any other way. Mario's ability to handle the Harrods presentation with minimal supervision contributed to the committee's positive assessment of him.

Chapter 9:   Letters that Document a Candidate's Volunteer Work

Some students distinguish themselves in the classroom, while others do so by pursuing a particular career path.   Yet other students fulfill their heartfelt potential – and make their maximum contribution to society – by volunteering for non-profit groups in their communities.   For these civic-minded candidates, it is imperative to submit a letter of recommendation from someone who can document these unique accomplishments.

A well-crafted letter from an administrator of a non-profit organization who can personally attest to your devotion to an outside cause will be highly perceived in the admissions process.   The letter should cite the specific contributions you have made to the organization; it should also emphasize your ability to get along with different types of people.   These references, if chosen wisely, can make your application unique and memorable.   They can also show that you have used your skills in an altruistic manner.

In paragraph 1:   The author should explain his/her relationship with you, including:

His/her title and employer
How long (s)he has known you
Your relationship to him/her
The nature (and extent) of your professional interactions

In paragraph 2 (and possibly 3):   The author should state his/her overall impression of you as a candidate.   Then, (s)he should mention the specific qualities that you have demonstrated in your interactions with him/her.   Remember, for business school recommendation letters, the power is in the details.   The author should explain:

a.   How you assisted the organization: teaching, mentoring, fundraising, organizing, recruiting, etc.
b.   Whether you supervised the work of others
c.   How many hours per week you devoted to the group

Ideally, the letter will also include specific examples to support the praise.   For example, if a letter claims that a candidate is a good writer, the author must mention a specific paper or assignment that the candidate completed in an extraordinary way.   What was the topic? The length?   What was terrific about the paper – was it short, concise, well documented, or unusually insightful?   Be specific.

In the next paragraph: All candidates, regardless of their background, are expected to demonstrate the general character traits that business schools value, which are listed on the rating scale.   They include:

a.   Intellectual curiosity, common sense
b.   Motivation, reliability, perseverance
c.   Judgment, resourcefulness, communication skills
d.   Interpersonal skills, emotional stability, self-confidence, empathy, maturity

Authors should document these points in the following paragraph, by mentioning the candidate's habits and relationships.   Is (s)he motivated, resourceful, and reliable?   Does (s)he require a lot of direction or very little?   Does (s)he coast by or constantly look for new ways to contribute?   Document it in the letter.   If possible, the author should also document the candidate's ability to work in a team environment.   Is (s)he a natural leader?   Did (s)he pull his/her weight on any team projects or presentations?   If so, offer specific details.

In the penultimate paragraph: Mention any other notable facts about the candidate that you want to convey.   This section of the letter has the most flexibility, depending upon the candidate's background and what you have personally observed.   Good points to include:

a.   Participation in outside activities related to a business career, including entrepreneurial ventures
b.   Devoting considerable time to the group, despite a full-time job (or demanding circumstances at home or school)

In the final paragraph: Authors should put their opinion of the candidate into the proper perspective.   How many volunteers have you supervised?   How does the candidate compare to the members of that group – is (s)he in the top 1%, 5%, or 20%?   If you have specific experience with candidates who have obtained an MBA, it is particularly helpful to compare the candidate to that group.   If the applicant is equally intelligent, motivated, and dynamic, this is the place to mention it.

In the closing statement: Offer a brief summary of the person's qualifications and state the strength of your recommendation (enthusiastic, without reservation, etc.). In the last sentence, you should provide your contact information (phone number and email address) in case the committee wants to confirm your letter or acquire additional details. Although it is highly unlikely that someone will contact you, your letter will have an added level of credibility if you make yourself accessible to the reader.

Finally, print your letter on your official letterhead and sign it as follows:

Lisa Chaffee	Name
Vice-President	Formal Title
Habitat for Humanity	Affiliation

Here are several recommendation letters for business school candidates that document their volunteer experiences. To protect the privacy of the writer and applicant, the names of all people, schools, places, and companies have been changed.

Letter #19: Volunteer for a Non-Profit Organization

For the past ten years, Danielle Davis has worked tirelessly for Cherished Children, a non-profit resource center for new mothers in the Milwaukee area. In 1999, Danielle was one of the first high school students to volunteer for us. In subsequent years, she continued to promote our organization in the tri-state area. After graduating from Northwestern University in 2008, Danielle put her education to work for us on a full-time basis when she became our Assistant Director of Community Services, which is a highly visible position in the Milwaukee community. As expected, she handles her myriad duties with maturity and confidence.

Looking back, I can't imagine that Cherished Children would have taken off, much less thrived, without Danielle's dedication and commitment. Over the years, she has eagerly accepted every challenge we presented to her, including seemingly impossible ones. At age sixteen, she solicited donations from local businesses in the community. On her own time, she scouted garage sales and flea markets for inexpensive baby furniture to give to our clients. When our grand opening was delayed for several days because of computer problems, she arranged for a local college student to fix the glitch at zero cost. Needless to say, Danielle quickly became the woman to see for a quick resolution to a million thorny problems.

Danielle's greatest strengths are her sensitivity and commitment to follow through. On more than one occasion, she has listened to our client's problems and taken the initiative to find a solution. Several of our most popular services, including well-baby care and Mommy & Me play dates, are a direct result of Danielle's suggestions. Fortunately, her commitment doesn't stop at the idea stage. Danielle is willing to do whatever is necessary to bring a needed service to the community, even if it means starting from scratch. No job is too big or too hard for her.

For the past two years, Danielle has worked diligently to create a breast cancer awareness program for Cherished Children. Last August, she negotiated a free mammography program with Milwaukee Community Hospital during National Breast Cancer Awareness Week. She also developed an hour-long educational seminar that she presents at local high schools, colleges and women's groups in the city. With her outgoing personality, Danielle is extremely effective at communicating the risks of the disease and the need for preventive examinations. She easily connects with the audience and spurs them to action.

Danielle's kindness and concern for others will undoubtedly serve her well in the future. I'm convinced that she has made such a great contribution to our group because people like her and trust her. They sense her enthusiasm for our cause and want to help us. After she graduates from business school, I can easily envision Danielle running a non-profit organization that provides quality health care to people in an underserved area. Based on her performance at Cherished Children, I can't imagine anyone better suited for the job.

Our Assessment: This letter provides an extensive, well-documented discussion of Danielle's commitment to a local non-profit organization. Thanks to this author, Danielle's independence, maturity and high energy level made a lasting impression on the admissions committee.

Letter #20: Launched a Non-Profit Organization

I have known Lisa Stanton since 2006, when we played together in the string section of the Seattle Symphony Orchestra.   At the time, Lisa was a college sophomore who was full of enthusiasm and ideas.   When she asked for my help in launching a non-profit organization to offer music lessons for inner-city children, I was apprehensive, but intrigued.   Lisa's passion for the idea soon won me over.   In August of 2007, we officially began to work on Music for Seattle.

Although Lisa didn't have any business experience, she was determined to make the program a success. Her first step was to contact local businesses to raise funds and to pitch the value of our program.   Lisa also researched various neighborhoods in Seattle to determine the ones that needed a productive after-school recreational activity for their children.   I often accompanied Lisa to local schools to try to raise awareness for Music for Seattle.   Although she was young, she had a clear voice and an innate persuasiveness.   Lisa was so enthusiastic and well-organized that people trusted her.   Within a matter of weeks, she convinced several local music teachers, along with a few of our peers in the Seattle Symphony Orchestra, to become volunteer instructors in the program.

Fundraising was a huge challenge, because we didn't have much money for supplies or expenses.   Lisa used her connections with the University of Portland to organize several fundraising events, including a holiday concert that raised $7,000 for Music for Seattle.   She also convinced her peers to hold car washes and bake sales, which added to our coffers.   Most importantly, Lisa persuaded a national instrument manufacturer to donate more than 200 used flutes, clarinets, and violins that they had taken in as trades.   As a seasoned fundraiser, I was impressed by Lisa's persistence, stamina, and creativity. She kept going long after most people would have given up.

Thanks to Lisa's efforts, we started our first set of classes in January of 2008.   By the following spring, we had 30 instructors teaching 150+ kids throughout the city.   I attribute our success mostly to Lisa's perseverance and my business direction.   From the start, everything we needed – time, money, instruments, and lessons - came from the goodness of people's hearts.   Lisa did everything possible to satisfy our contributors.   Every week, she tracked and reported all of our spending on our public web site.   Lisa also made efficient use of our limited resources.   Over time, she formed strong relationships with our benefactors and volunteers, who felt a certain sense of loyalty to our cause.   By 2009, our reputation in Seattle was so strong that we attracted the attention of a national news outlet, which broadcast a story about us.   They also put a donation link on their web site, which attracted $50,000 in donations from caring viewers.   This generous sum was enough to pay for a long-term lease on our downtown facility.

In December of 2009, I ended my formal affiliation with Music for Seattle when I moved to New York City for business.   By this time, Lisa had outgrown his need for my direction, and easily kept it going in my absence. Indeed, Music for Seattle would not exist without her passion and generosity.

In creating and running Music for Seattle, Lisa has already cultivated many leadership attributes; she is focused, compassionate, and willing to take calculated risks.   Lisa is also an excellent manager who can satisfy the needs of different groups of stakeholders.   She instinctively understands how to work efficiently with a limited budget.

As the Senior Vice President of Radio City Music Hall, I work with dozens of talented young managers. Lisa is an outstanding young woman, clearly in the top 1% of all MBAs I have known.   Since we first met in 2006, she has matured into a successful professional with a passion for public service.   I am certain that Lisa will bring the same tenacity and exuberance to business school that she brought to Music for Seattle.

Our Assessment: Although he does not identify himself until the final paragraph, this author is a highly-recognized leader in the entertainment industry.   His willingness to mentor Lisa and endorse her so positively in a reference letter gave Lisa's essay about the music program enhanced credibility.   The committee was also impressed by what this letter DIDN'T say.   Rather than try to editorialize on the candidate's academic fit for an MBA program, the author restricted his comments to his own interactions with Lisa.   As a result, they knew that this letter wasn't forced or coached, which made its contents even more reliable.   Fortunately, Lisa also submitted strong letters from academic references who validated her academic excellence.

Letter #21:   Educational Advocate

Please accept this letter as my enthusiastic endorsement of Ms. Janet Lin, who serves as the Director of Fundraising and Support Services for International Educational Equality, a non-profit entity that I founded in 2007.

Three years ago, I met Janet for the first time at an alumni meeting for our alma mater, Shanghai University.   At the time, she had a prestigious career as a financial analyst at Bank of America and devoted her free time to volunteer initiatives in the Asian-American community.   I thoroughly enjoyed our discussions, which revealed Janet's passion for helping immigrant children.   When I offered her a position at Educational Equality, I never dreamed that she would accept. To my delight, Janet was more than willing to join a fledgling non-profit group that improved the lives of Asian-Americans.

From the minute she joined our organization, Janet became a tireless fundraiser and advocate in the community. Within weeks, she had solicited donations from several local businesses that serve the Bay Area's burgeoning Asian-American population.   She also formed partnerships with other non-profit organizations that could help us provide tutoring services in the Oakland and San Francisco school systems.   Despite the obvious challenges, Janet was convinced that we could improve the students' lives by offering them a quality education.

Within her first month at International Educational Equality, Janet revealed her amazing strengths as an English as a Second Language (ESL) teacher.   Although her students had varying literacy levels when they entered the program, thanks to Janet, they achieved a 90% retention rate of their basic English terms, which is nothing short of extraordinary.   From the start, Janet created a supportive and respectful classroom atmosphere, which empowered her students to succeed.   She immediately took three high school girls under her wing and tutored them in their studies.   Within a month, they raised their class averages from an F to a C and gained a strong sense of self-confidence.   Since then, these recent immigrants, who were struggling to assimilate into American culture, have continued to improve in the classroom.   With Janet's encouragement, they have opened their minds to the possibility of a college education and a professional future in the United States.

Yet Janet was not content to simply teach language classes at International Educational Equality.   With the support of our staff, she expanded our curriculum to include practical information the students could use in their daily lives. On her own initiative, Janet pioneered the development of classes such as Landlord and Tenant Relationships, Understanding the Electoral Process, and Gaining Access to Health Care, to apprise the students of their benefits and rights.   Because of their practical nature, these classes have become extremely popular with Asian-American families in the community.

Janet's fluency in Spanish, Mandarin, Korean, and English enables her to communicate with a diverse population. More impressively, she not only speaks many languages, but connects emotionally with a variety of people and situations.   As a child, Janet was separated from her parents for several years due to their problems obtaining a work visa in the U.S.   As a result, she lived alone with her grandmother in Oakland, who barely spoke a word of English.   By adapting to her new environment without familial support, Janet became an independent woman with a passion to help others.   When I first met her at the alumni meeting, Janet was ready to channel her career onto a path that offered long-term benefits to the community.

As her peer, I am touched by Janet's compassion for children and her unflagging sense of idealism.   There is no doubt in my mind that she has the intelligence and drive to develop effective programs to improve the educational offerings for immigrant children. You will be lucky to have a student with her maturity and commitment.

Our Assessment: This candidate made a jarring career change when she left the financial world to work at a non-profit group.   Although she discussed her decision in her personal statement, she could not tell the full story in just two pages.   This letter complements her statement in a positive way and gives the reader a better understanding of who Janet is.   It also reveals her strengths as a fundraiser, teacher, and community advocate.

Letter #22: Peace Corps Volunteer

For the past twenty-three years, I have served as the Director of Volunteers for the West African Relief Division of the Peace Corps. During that time, I have recruited, trained and supervised nearly two thousand volunteers from numerous professional disciplines and nearly all walks of life. Few have impressed me more than Shawna O'Conner, who served as a teacher in Ghana between 2006 and 2008. I hired Shawna and was her direct supervisor throughout her two years of service. After working closely with her under extraordinary circumstances, I feel well qualified to comment on numerous aspects of her personal and professional stature.

Shawna was one of the most productive, caring and effective workers I've had the pleasure of knowing. Prior to her Peace Corps participation, she obtained her BA in Education and had several years of professional experience teaching high school English. Shawna possessed an abundance of skills, including language fluency, experience in educational program development, and a willingness to teach in an economically challenged area. After careful consideration, Shawna willingly gave up the security of Emporia, Kansas to work in a small West African village.

Her mission was to establish an effective curriculum in the community's newly established public school system. Although the building and utilities were adequate, the school lacked teachers with bilingual skills and experience in teaching older students. They also lacked essential supplies, including computers and software packages that we take for granted in the United States. Shawna's group brought the essential supplies to the school and trained the staff in how to use them efficiently.

Shawna's primary achievement was implementing new teaching methods for English, math and reading classes. Not surprisingly, the language barrier and hygiene issues presented difficult barriers for the students and volunteers alike. The teachers were particularly challenged by sexism. Ghana still does not acknowledge the educational rights of women; they also disapprove of women in leadership roles. Nevertheless, Shawna did everything possible to help her female students, whose families did not support their efforts to become educated and self-sufficient. She encouraged all of her students to not simply dream of a better life, but to create it for themselves by completing their education.

Shawna was a wonderful role model who earned the community's respect and support. She also achieved impressive results. During Shawna's tenure in Ghana, the dropout rate decreased by 46% and the teenage literacy rate increased by 29%. Over time, the newly-built school enrolled more students and eventually served two neighboring villages.

Shawna was an integral part of the group's success. She was also a joy to work with. She is compassionate, kind and highly sensitive to the needs of her students. Even during times of illness, Shawna remained committed to her job. Consequently, I'm certain that she can handle the challenges of business school.

Shawna is a natural leader with a passion to make a difference. Amazingly, she also remains committed to our international relief efforts. Since leaving the Peace Corps, Shawna has written several training manuals for the school in Ghana and has offered creative suggestions for its expansion. As a volunteer, she ranks among the top 1% of the thousands I have worked with. I recommend her without reservation for any type of assignment.

<u>Our Assessment</u>: In business school admissions, candidates with experience in international relief work have a strong competitive edge. By serving a disadvantaged population, they develop the dedication and communication skills that are required in most executive positions. This particular letter does an excellent job of documenting Shawna's Peace Corps work. It also validates her integrity as a human being. The author is a noted leader whose observations were highly respected by the admissions committee. He has a reputation for being a demanding boss who expects 110% from his volunteers. Once again, this is an excellent example of having the right author confirm your strengths in a simple, honest manner.

Letter #23: Election Volunteer

How long have you known the applicant and in what capacity?

I first met Ms. Glenda Ryan in 1998, when she worked on Senator Joseph Chaffee's election campaign in Portland, Oregon.   At the time, I was the Deputy Mayor of Portland and the Chairman of the Oregon Chapter of the Republican Party.   For most of the year, I campaigned aggressively for Senator Chaffee's election, which allowed me to work closely with Glenda.   For the 1998 election, Glenda's primary responsibilities were conducting research, organizing rallies, and maintaining our computer database.   Although she was one of our youngest staff members, she was incredibly passionate and reliable.

Since then, Glenda and I have collaborated on Senator Chaffee's two subsequent election campaigns in 2004 and 2010, in which he won nearly 70% of the popular vote.   During that time, Glenda's responsibilities have expanded dramatically.   For the 2004 election, Glenda advanced to the role of volunteer coordinator, which required her to recruit, train, and supervise dozens of volunteers in the Portland office.   Based on her impressive commitment and performance, Glenda was offered a paid position for the 2010 campaign, which required her to coordinate the work of 300 volunteers at 12 different offices in Oregon.   Her subsequent performance was nothing short of extraordinary.

How do you assess the applicant's leadership potential and integrity?

When I first met Glenda in 1998, I was immediately impressed by her focus and commitment.   Although she was still in high school, she was extremely knowledgeable about the political process and deeply invested in the state's future.   Senator Chaffee's liberal policies on health care and immigration resonated strongly with Glenda, which sparked her desire to contribute.   During the 2004 campaign, Glenda had just completed her degree at Stanford, where she majored in Political Science and lobbied strongly for the local Republican Party.   As a result, she brought an impressive combination of organizational and interpersonal skills, along with a mature perspective of the state political scene, to Senator Chaffee's 2004 and 2010 campaigns.

With her excellent organizational skills, Glenda excelled at her myriad responsibilities, including conducting polls, scheduling volunteers, negotiating with vendors, arranging for publicity, and writing speeches, phone scripts, and press releases.   For complex tasks, Glenda had a knack for assigning the right people to the right jobs, which made our campaigns more efficient.   She also diffused many conflicts between staff members by keeping them focused on their common goal.   With her stellar leadership skills, Glenda has a bright future in the Oregon political scene.

Based on your experience with this applicant, please describe his/her level of enthusiasm/energy. Please provide some examples.

Glenda works tirelessly to help the members of our community, both through her job an on her own time.   Besides her work for our campaigns, Glenda also volunteers at the Portland Sharing Center, which is a non-profit group that serves women and children who are victims of domestic violence.   Whenever possible, Glenda helps them find shelter and file the paperwork for a restraining order.   She also negotiates on their behalf with landlords, employers, and utility companies.   By fighting for the rights of innocent parties, Glenda has earned the trust of countless people in our community.

Please assess this candidate's ability to work effectively in teams.

From my perspective, Glenda's greatest strength is her power of persuasion.   In Senator Chaffee's campaigns, we faced considerable opposition from constituents who opposed his support of the Iraqi war and his conservative position on gay rights and national health care.   To win the support of Independent voters, we needed to communicate the Senator's message clearly, concisely, and persuasively to various audiences.   Not surprisingly, we encountered many angry and stubborn people on the campaign trail who rejected our platform and challenged our commitment to our cause.   It was Glenda's job to reach those people and convince them that Senator Chaffee would do an excellent job on their behalf.   She did it better than anyone I have ever seen.

Throughout the campaigns, Glenda listened compassionately to our constituents' concerns and addressed them in her speeches and press releases.   She also held her own in political discussions with people who were significantly older than she was.   By being focused and respectful, Glenda made her points and won the trust of our constituents.   In 2004, Senator Chaffee won the support of more than 75% of Independent voters.   He could never have done so without Glenda's aggressive campaigning on his behalf.

In what areas does the applicant need the most improvement?

With formal training in business, Glenda will have a greater understanding of the financial aspects of campaigns, which will enable her to assume additional responsibilities at the state level.

Additional Comments:

Glenda is one of the most intelligent, passionate, and effective people I know.   She will be a tremendous asset to her business school class.

Our Assessment: The author of this letter is a distinguished leader in the Republican Party, who rarely endorses candidates for business school.   His willingness to do so in such a detailed and enthusiastic manner was a testament to Glenda's character and skills.   By taking the time to discuss her evolution over time, including her work for the Portland Sharing Center, he gave Glenda's application the boost it needed it a highly competitive applicant pool.

Chapter 10: Letters for Candidates with Advanced Degrees

Although most business school applicants are recent college graduates, some have advanced degrees in other disciplines. Within this group, many candidates also have several years of relevant work experience. For these applicants, a powerful letter of recommendation, which highlights their unique intellectual accomplishments, is an essential part of the application package.

In most respects, reference letters for candidates with advanced degrees are no different than those for other applicants – they should be written and organized in the same way that we described in Chapters 6 – 9. The only difference is that the committee may wonder why the candidate is seeking an MBA after obtaining an advanced degree in an alternative field. If the author can provide this insight as part of his/her letter, it can complement and reinforce the material in the candidate's essays. Ideally, the letter will also confirm the candidate's personal and professional fit for a business career.

Otherwise, the letter should adhere to the same principles we have reiterated throughout this publication. It should:

1. Describe the author's relationship with the candidate
2. Highlight the academic, professional, and personal strengths that the writer has personally observed
3. Support every claim with an example or anecdote
4. Compare the candidate to others in his/her peer group

Here are several recommendation letters for business school candidates who have already completed advanced degrees in other areas. To protect the privacy of the writer and applicant, the names of all people, classes, schools, places, and companies have been changed.

Letter #24:   Candidate with an Advanced Degree

It is with great pleasure that I endorse Rose Marie Randall's application to your program.   For the last 30 years at Brown University, I have been a Clinical Psychologist and Department Head of the Counseling and Student Development Center, as well as the supervisor to many interns and social work students.   I hope that my perspective will be helpful to you as you evaluate this exceptional candidate.

My first contact with Rose Marie was during the summer of 1997, when, as an undergraduate student at Brown, she volunteered to lead a summer conference in Providence for teenagers with learning disabilities.   At the time, Rose Marie was a senior in college who was full of enthusiasm for her first "real job." During the course of the week, Rose Marie presented the material with such ease and humor that she set the tone for the entire workshop. Her creative ideas for presentations and activities were inventive and entertaining; they were also highly effective.

With children from a variety of backgrounds, there were occasional conflicts.   Rose Marie always responded with respect and compassion, while setting appropriate limits.   The experience had a profound effect on the children. Because of Rose Marie's exceptional skill and professionalism, she was invited by many schools to offer similar workshops

After her graduation in 2000, Rose Marie subsequently completed both her M.A. and Ph.D. in Social Work at Brown. During that time, she has demonstrated a true talent for working with disabled children.   Regardless of her heavy academic load, she has also distinguished herself as a conscientious and energetic volunteer.   I have enormous respect for her teaching and leadership skills, and have been pleased to work with her on many occasions.

Two years ago, Rose Marie was asked to develop a summer program for teenagers with learning disabilities at Boston University.   As Department Head, I was honored to have one of my graduate students selected to develop such a highly visible program.   Rose Marie's skills as a mentor, teacher and friend quickly won the admiration of the students and administrators in Boston.   She led group discussions and facilitated role-plays with great skill, and also helped in the development of outreach programs.   Rose Marie is particularly gifted at identifying students' needs, encouraging their contributions, and involving them in the planning process.   Her commitment and passion for her work was evident throughout the summer program.

Rose Marie's true passion is the development of Federally-subsidized programs for children with dyslexia and Attention Deficit Hyperactivity Disorder (A.D.H.D.).   Many times, the availability of help in a child's local school system is the primary predictor of his/her eventual success.   Unfortunately, students in large cities (with high tax bases) continue to receive the lion's share of the available resources, while students from rural areas and under-funded school systems (through no fault of their own) tend to lag behind.   I strongly suspect that Rose Marie's motivation to attend business school is to become an advocate for the students and families who lack a voice in the current system.   As someone who has worked diligently to develop programs for learning-disabled children, Rose Marie is determined to bring them to every student in the United States.

Rose Marie is a gifted educator who has much to offer a top-tier MBA program.   I have the greatest admiration for her work and her dedication to others.   Your program sounds ideally suited to Rose Marie's talents; if accepted, she will bring a decade of experience in academic research and program development, along with a powerful combination of interpersonal strengths (dedication, maturity, compassion and integrity).   She also has a profound enthusiasm for learning and teaching, as well as a resolute desire to understand new theories and ideas. I urge you to carefully consider Rose Marie Randall who is, quite simply, the most remarkable teacher I have ever met.

<u>Our Assessment</u>:   This is an exceptional letter about an exceptional candidate.   The author provides a detailed discussion of Rose Marie's strengths as a student, teacher and advocate.   As a result, the committee understood her motivation for pursuing a business degree at this stage in her career.   Furthermore, Rose Marie's goal of working in the non-profit arena was an excellent fit for her background and skills.   Her application was well-perceived.

Letter #25: Candidate with an Advanced Degree

How long have you known the applicant and in what capacity?

I am honored to write a letter of recommendation on behalf of Mr. Heinrich Stow, who has applied for admission to business school. Between 2004 and 2008, I served as his graduate research advisor at the University of Georgia, where I am a Professor of Chemistry. After observing Heinrich in the classroom and laboratory, I feel well qualified to assess the many skills that he will bring to business school.

How do you assess the applicant's leadership potential and integrity?

Before he enrolled in the Ph. D. program at the University of Georgia, Heinrich completed his B.S. and M.S. degrees in Chemistry at Kansas State University, where he developed a novel polymer coating for the food industry. As a result of this experience, Heinrich brought exemplary analytical and problem solving skills to our program. At UGA, Heinrich focused on the development of an edible type of shellac for use in the confectionary industry, to prevent the "bleeding" of peanut butter and caramel into chocolate coating. After a few false starts, he achieved considerable success with Compound X, for which he was awarded a U.S. Patent. Later, in 2007, Heinrich received a second patent for the processing method for Compound X, which he recently licensed to the Nestle Corporation for an impressive sum.

During his time at UGA, Heinrich's greatest achievement was completing his dissertation for his Ph.D. project, along with two patent applications for his inventions. To do so, Heinrich documented his research in painstaking detail, including several diagrams that conveyed technical information in an understandable way. His subsequent dissertation was one of the most succinct, informative, and insightful documents I have seen.

For his oral defense, Heinrich prepared a professional set of Power Point slides that detailed the theoretical analysis of his research; he also distributed a booklet of relevant material to his committee members. As his advisor, I was highly impressed by the quality of Heinrich's work and his meticulous attention to detail. I have rarely observed a more practical and well-organized student.

Based on your experience with this applicant, please describe his/her level of enthusiasm/energy. Please provide some examples.

Throughout his program at UGA, Heinrich completed several rigorous courses in food processing, engineering and statistics. He excelled in his higher level coursework and obtained perfect scores on his written qualifier exam and oral research exam, which required him to master extremely complex topics. Despite his heavy workload, Heinrich was always eager to discuss new ideas that would enhance the quality of his work. More than any other student, he was invigorated by the challenges his research presented.

Please assess this candidate's ability to work effectively in teams.

Heinrich is a pleasant man who built positive relationships with his fellow students and the members of his doctoral committee. In departmental meetings, he was thoughtful, courteous and constructive. Whenever asked, he would share information with his fellow students and help them with their projects. Based on his performance at UGA, where he was a popular and successful student, I would rate him as an excellent team player.

As a doctoral candidate at UGA, Heinrich also proved to be an articulate and popular teacher. For his introductory laboratory course in chemistry, Heinrich conducted numerous demonstrations based on his students' interests. He went well beyond our expectations to get the class interested in – and comfortable with – basic chemical principles. At the end of the semester, I received overwhelmingly positive feedback from the students about Heinrich's enthusiastic teaching style, which reflected well on our entire department.

In what areas does the applicant need the most improvement?

After completing his doctorate at UGA, Heinrich accepted a position as the Director of Research at Sugar and Spice Confectionary, where he continues to expand his line of candy coatings. In this capacity, he manages a group of five scientists and technicians who conduct basic research and experimental line trials. To advance his career, Heinrich must balance his technical expertise with formal training in business, including classes in finance and strategy. Afterwards, Heinrich will have the knowledge and skills he will need to advance to the executive level in a global confectionary firm.   The program at XXX, which is known for its quantitative rigor, is an excellent match for Heinrich's analytical skills and flair for innovation.

Additional Comments:

After working with him on a professional basis, I am certain that Heinrich possesses the intelligence, motivation, and organizational skills that are required to succeed in business school.   I offer him my strongest recommendation.

<u>Our Assessment</u>:   This letter provides powerful documentation of the candidates' skills as a researcher and innovator.   Among a highly competitive applicant pool, his accomplishments in his doctoral program set him apart from the crowd – and earned him a seat in the class.

Letter #26: Candidate with an Advanced Degree

How long have you know the applicant and in what connection? If applicable, briefly describe the applicant's role in your organization. Please comment on the frequency of your interaction. (250 word limit)

I have known Dr. Charles DeCosta for nine years in my position as the Head of Oncology at St. Mary's Hospital in Madrid, Spain.   I supervised Dr. DeCosta's dissertation research, which he completed as part of his M.D./Ph.D. program at the University of Madrid.   Charles researched the impact of smoking in premenopausal patients with ovarian cancer, which required him to assimilate a large quantity of contradictory information before he conducted his laboratory work and analyzed his data.

Charles explored this complex subject with unusual insight, which allowed him to drive his research forward. He hypothesized that women who smoked were far more likely to be diagnosed with ovarian cancer before age 30 because the nicotine triggered a unique beta cell reaction in the pancreas.   The resulting change in the levels of two pancreatic enzymes could therefore be used as an early indicator of ovarian cancer. This novel theory, which was eloquent in its simplicity, had never been explored in a clinical setting.

Although I was available in an advisory capacity, Dr. DeCosta performed and executed all of the research and statistical analyses with minimal guidance.   Then, he summarized his results in a comprehensive thesis, which was accepted by the standing medical committee at the University of Madrid.   Dr. DeCosta's research has brought us a step closer to understanding the impact of smoking on patients with ovarian cancer, which is one of the most deadly malignancies of our time.

What do you consider the applicant's talents or strengths? (250 word limit)

A creative and analytical thinker, Dr. DeCosta excels at all aspects of medical research.   His thesis required a mastery of oncology, molecular biology, gynecology, and clinical medicine.   From the start, Charles showed an amazing ability to extract the salient points from conflicting pieces of literature and bring his laboratory results into the proper context to research a novel hypothesis.   Throughout the project, Dr. DeCosta handled setbacks with intelligence and ease.   When he encountered an obstacle, Charles had the maturity to re-evaluate his situation and bring fresh insight to his work.   Dr. DeCosta's ability to plan, organize and steer his research enabled him to complete an impressive amount of work in a short period of time.

Since completing his medical degree, Dr. DeCosta has built a successful practice treating gynecological cancers at the University of Barcelona Medical Center, where he continues to investigate the role of smoking in the disease process.   A year ago, he also launched a freestanding clinic that offers early screenings for breast, cervical, and colon cancer for the residents of Barcelona.   Through this venture, Charles has flexed his skills as an entrepreneur in an area of personal and professional significance to him.   His superior skills as a physician, combined with his ability to take a calculated risk, have reaped great rewards.   They will invariably serve Charles well in business school.

What do you consider the applicant's weaknesses or developmental needs? (250 word limit)

When he first joined my group, Charles was overly confident in his reasoning and occasionally jumped to an incorrect conclusion.   Rather than discuss the issue with me – and possibly refine his thoughts – he proceeded with projects before he obtained adequate background information.   As a result, Charles occasionally had to re-evaluate the situation and repeat parts of his work.

After I discussed this weakness with Charles, he immediately took several steps to address it.   When he was excited about an idea, he solicited my opinion before he commenced his work.   Then, he listened to constructive suggestions and incorporated them into his plans.   In ambiguous situations, Charles conducted a small analysis to test and refine a theory before he advanced to a larger scale investigation.   As a result, he generated better proposals with a greater likelihood of success.

What industry / function might best suit this individual, and what do you see this person doing in ten years? Why? (250 word limit)

Dr. DeCosta's unusual combination of training and skills will provide him with many choices in his professional future.   With his academic training, he is already well-suited for a career in teaching, research, and clinical medicine.   Further, his recent experience launching the health care clinic suggests a definite entrepreneurial flair.   Recently, when he requested this letter, Dr. DeCosta expressed his desire to assume a leadership role in health care development and administration, which will allow him to bring quality care to patients in developing parts of the world.   With formal training in management, Dr. DeCosta will be well-prepared to achieve this objective.

The predominant teaching method at XXXXX Business School is case-based learning. It is a highly interactive experience requiring the proficient use of English-reading, speaking, listening, writing and integrating "real time." Please comment on the applicant's ability to contribute to this learning model. (250 word limit)

Dr. DeCosta's warmth and intelligence are paralleled by his exceptional communication skills.   After living and working on several continents, he is equally comfortable reading, speaking and writing in three different languages.   In clinical settings, Charles also possesses the emotional intelligence to handle the human aspects of medicine.   Throughout his academic career, his exemplary behavior set a positive example for his fellow students.

In a group environment, Charles is a team player who is willing to help those with less experience.   He thrived in research discussion groups, in which he offered good suggestions to his peers and accepted criticism in a constructive manner.   From all indications, he will thrive in XXXXX's highly interactive, "real time" environment.

The XXXXX Business School is committed to developing outstanding leaders who can inspire trust and confidence in other. Please comment on the applicant's behavior (e.g., respect for others, honesty, integrity, accountability for personal behavior) within your organization and in the community. (250 word limit)

Dr. DeCosta is an exceptional man who is committed to serving others.   Throughout his academic and professional careers, he has demonstrated exemplary moral behavior, which has inspired the trust of his patients and peers.   In clinical settings, Charles is a compassionate doctor who puts the needs of his patients first.   In all aspects of his work, he protects the confidentiality of his patients and he expects others to do the same.   In an area like clinical research, in which patient privacy is paramount, Charles displays a level of integrity that is beyond reproach.

In addition to his professional strengths, I am equally impressed by Dr. DeCosta's impeccable sense of empathy. On his own initiative, he provided medical support after the terrorist attack on our train system, which allowed him to save hundreds of lives.   His goal of improving health care delivery in an underserved area also reveals an inherent level of selflessness.   In character and performance, Dr. DeCosta demonstrates the requisite integrity to lead an international organization.   I recommend him without hesitation for admission to XXXXX Business School.

Our Assessment: As always, the strength of the letter is in the details.   Every point is supported by a concrete example that puts the observation into its proper context.   This letter also provides an eloquent discussion of the candidate's skills as a physician, researcher, and entrepreneur, which would allow him to bring a novel perspective to the class.

Chapter 11: Letters for Older and Non-Traditional Candidates

Although most business school applicants are recent college graduates, some have significant experience in their respective fields of study. For these candidates, a powerful letter of recommendation, which highlights their maturity, focus, and professional track record, is an essential part of the application package.

In most respects, reference letters for older and non-traditional candidates are no different than those for other applicants – they should be written and organized in the same way that we described in Chapters 6 – 9. For older candidates, this is a golden opportunity to update the committee on what you have accomplished since you graduated from college. Your reference letters should explain the type and extent of your professional experiences and how they have influenced your goals. Ideally, your supervisor can provide considerable insight into your career progression, including the cultivation of previously unknown talents and skills.

Additionally, the committee will may wonder why the candidate is seeking a business degree after working for many years in another profession. If the author can provide this insight as part of his/her letter, it can complement and reinforce the material in the candidate's application essays. Ideally, the letter will also confirm the candidate's personal and professional fit for a business career.

Otherwise, the letter should adhere to the same principles we have reiterated throughout this publication. It should:

1. Describe the author's relationship with the candidate
2. Highlight the academic, professional, and personal strengths that the writer has personally observed
3. Support every claim with an example or anecdote
4. Compare the candidate to others in his/her peer group

Here are several recommendation letters for business school candidates who have already worked for several years in another profession. To protect the privacy of the writer and applicant, the names of all people, classes, schools, places, and companies have been changed.

Letter #27: Older and Non-Traditional Candidate

I am honored to write a letter of recommendation on behalf of Virginia Godfrey, who is a candidate for admission to XXXXX Business School. As an attorney, I have supervised Ginny for ten years at Oregon Protection and Advocacy (OPA), where she works as an investigator.

OPA is a federally-funded, non-profit law office whose primary mission is to advance and defend the rights of patients with mental illness. As an investigator, Ginny ensures that local hospitals provide quality care according to the relevant state and federal laws. Without exception, she has demonstrated an impressive ability to read, analyze and apply complex regulations to her large case load. I am consistently impressed by Ginny's ability to thrive in a stressful and often thankless position. Despite the low pay, high turnover and persistent lack of resources, her commitment to our clients is unshakable.

Since Ginny first became an investigator in 2000, she has won over 90 social security disability cases that several seasoned attorneys claimed "had no merit." Her written and oral arguments were nothing short of brilliant. Ginny has a sharp mind, a keen attention to detail, and an ability to anticipate and solve potential barriers to her arguments. As a result, she is as sharp in the courtroom as most attorneys.

To survive in such a high pressure environment, Ginny must juggle dozens of responsibilities at once without "dropping a ball" or mis-prioritizing her workload. When necessary, she will go far beyond what is expected of her to serve her clients. In 2004, Ginny took the initiative to write and publish a 150-page manual for people who were trying to obtain social services in Oregon. The document, which was written in an informative, easy-to-read style, has been a valuable resource for citizens throughout the state.

With her exceptional communication skills, Ginny is also a natural leader and teacher. In her ten years with OPA, she has presented numerous state-wide training sessions for judges, lawyers, advocates, law enforcement personnel and mental health professionals. By nature, Ginny welcomes these experiences as a chance to learn more about the community's needs. By taking questions from the audience and probing their concerns, Ginny has found creative ways to fill the gaps in our social services system.

Ginny's salient strength is her ability to work cooperatively with an amazingly diverse group of people. Because our organization works under a federal mandate to oversee psychiatric hospitals and facilities, Ginny's predecessors often had an adversarial relationship with the employees at these locations. By emphasizing their collective goal of providing exemplary care to patients with mental illness, Ginny developed a strong rapport with health care providers across the state.

Ginny has also earned the trust and respect of the patients she serves. On one occasion, Ginny represented a severely disturbed woman who was facing involuntary commitment. During the course of the proceeding, the woman began to make threats and scream at the judge. When the bailiffs tried to restrain the woman, Ginny immediately turned them away, because she knew that their intervention would escalate the situation and potentially cause harm. Within minutes, Ginny gained control of an unsafe situation by utilizing her profound interpersonal skills and the trust that she had cultivated with her client. The woman was subsequently committed without resistance.

In my 20-year career as an attorney, I have never met anyone with the dedication, perseverance or compassion of Virginia Godfrey; she is one of our community's most valuable assets. Please contact me at (phone number) or at XXXXXX@host.net if you require further elaboration.

<u>Our Assessment:</u> This author, who is a nationally known attorney, did an excellent job of crediting Ginny with many accomplishments as an advocate. Since Ginny had worked for ten years for the same social service organization, the committee benefited greatly from hearing the author's perspective.

Letter #28: Older and Non-Traditional Candidate

I am pleased to write a letter of recommendation on behalf of Sophia Davis-Stowe, who is an extraordinary student and linguist. I have known Sophia since September of 2003 in my position as a Professor of Foreign Languages at the University of Chicago. Beginning in the fall semester of that year, Sophia began the ambitious task of completing a triple major in Spanish, Mandarin, and Arabic, which had never been attempted at UC. In the next four years, I was privileged to watch this amazing woman complete this herculean task with excellent grades. Her performance and commitment were nothing short of miraculous.

During her sophomore and junior years, I taught three of Sophia's classes: *Mandarin I, II, and III* (lectures plus labs). She also completed my summer class entitled *Mandarin in Business and Commerce*, which presents a formidable challenge for most students because it requires an extensive amount of reading in an abbreviated timeframe. Before the first day of class, Sophia took the initiative to read one of the required texts. As a result, she was well prepared for the volume and intensity of the material.

In subsequent weeks, Sophia proved to be an exemplary student – she arrived on time for every class and was well prepared to discuss the reading assignments with her peers. Although many students did not grasp the nuances of Chinese laws, including the controversial "one child" policy, Sophia easily comprehended this topic because she had lived in China for most of her childhood. As a result, she brought a seasoned perspective to our discussions about humanitarian concerns, immigration issues, and intellectual property disputes.

Sophia was a gracious contributor who stated her opinions clearly and respectfully. She also listened patiently to others and kept an open mind about alternative viewpoints. More than any other student, she stayed abreast of world news, and had an impressive command of current events in Asia and the Middle East. Although morning classes are notoriously difficult in the summer, Sophia's high energy level always kept the class stimulated. She was – and remains – one of my favorite students.

In all of my classes, Sophia worked diligently to stay abreast of the material and earn top grades on my exams, which were usually in essay format. Despite the rigid time limit, Sophia provided clear, concise, and well-organized answers to every question. She was one of the few students to meet my high standards, which were admittedly quite high.

Sophia's performance is particularly impressive, considering that she was working 40 hours per week throughout her four years at UC. Although this exhausting schedule placed considerable demands on Sophia, who is the sole support for her elderly parents, she managed to stay on track and complete a triple major. As her professor, I applaud her dedication and tenacity, along with her willingness to create a better life for herself.

At 39, Sophia is older and more mature than the typical business school candidate. As a result, she brings a sense of confidence and purpose to her studies that few applicants possess. With her passion for languages, business, and politics, I am certain that Sophia will achieve her goal of running a global business. I offer her my strongest - and most enthusiastic - support.

Our Assessment: This distinguished professor eloquently explained the unique strengths that this "late bloomer" would bring to business school. After reading about her exceptional work ethic and language skills, the committee knew that this was a special candidate who would add significant diversity to the classroom.

Letter #29: Older and Non-Traditional Candidate

How long have you known the applicant and in what capacity?

Please accept this letter as my enthusiastic support for my former employee, Simon Horowicz. In the fall of 2000, Simon became a Medical Recruiter at Health Care Solutions, where I am the Senior Vice President. Over the next five years, we worked closely on several placements for job candidates in the San Francisco Bay area.

Although it was Simon's first job after college, he quickly made a positive impact on our company. As a Medical Recruiter, Simon had to decipher complicated requirements for each position and find a creative way to fill them with qualified candidates. Thankfully, Simon proved to be fast learner with a scrupulous attention to detail. Many times, he worked on multiple openings with very different professional requirements. By organizing his data about potential candidates and positions for immediate retrieval, Simon became successful a lot faster than his peers.

What is the applicant's greatest strength? Please give an example.

Simon's greatest skill was his ability to "read" candidates and determine their fit for a particular hospital or medical center. During an interview, he asked perceptive questions and listened carefully to the candidate's responses. Many times, Simon elicited important information that we would otherwise have missed. From my experience, this type of emotional intelligence is extremely rare – and cannot easily be taught. In Simon's case, it allowed him to make savvy and efficient decisions about candidates, which were later verified by reference checks.

Please describe the applicant's greatest accomplishment.

I was particularly impressed by the proactive way that Simon located qualified candidates. In our industry, we teach our recruiters to utilize Internet User Groups as a way to connect with job seekers in the medical field. Once he started, Simon took the process a step further than anyone else. He identified nearly one thousand employees of local hospitals, HMOs and PPOs and divided them by job function (physician, nurse, administrator, technician, etc.). Then, Simon contacted the most desirable candidates to determine their interest in changing jobs. This simple step gave him immediate access to a pool of candidates who were "outside the radar" of our competitors. This type of creative thinking and initiative are what made Simon exceptional.

In 2003, Simon advanced to the level of Senior Recruiter with Health Care Solutions. In this role, he filled several top-tier clinical, research, and executive positions at San Francisco Memorial Hospital, which was a highly lucrative account for us. His exceptional performance attracted the attention of several competitive firms, including Med-U-Call, Inc., which lured him away from us in 2005 with an unbeatable compensation package. Although I was sorry to see Simon go, I was excited to see the mature and successful professional that he had become. As expected, Simon continues to excel in all aspects of medical recruiting and management, despite the downturn in the economy.

In what area does the applicant need improvement?

With an MBA, Simon will have the skills he needs to launch his own recruiting firm in the health care industry. Formal training in business and strategy will be invaluable to him in at this stage of his career.

Is there anything else we should know about the applicant?

As the Senior Vice President of a successful recruiting firm, I like to think that I have good instincts about people – and what they can accomplish. In all areas of evaluation, Simon Horowicz consistently exceeded my expectations and set the standard of excellence for his peers. He will undoubtedly make a great contribution to his MBA program.

Our Assessment: At first blush, the committee did not understand why this candidate was willing to leave an extremely lucrative job to enroll in business school. This recommendation letter, in conjunction with the candidate's application essays, illuminated his longstanding interest in health care and the organizational skills he would bring to the program. It also documented his impressive career trajectory in a highly competitive field, which distinguished him from other candidates.

Chapter 12:   Candidates with International Experience

Not surprisingly, candidates with international work experience – and a global perspective of business – are highly prized in the admissions process.   If possible, these candidates should present a recommendation letter that documents their familiarity with others languages, cultures, and business practices.   Ideally, the letter should also cite the candidate's ability to build and lead cross-functional, cross-cultural project teams, which is the underlying goal of many top-tier MBA programs.

Otherwise, the letter should adhere to the same principles we have reiterated throughout this publication.   It should:

1.   Describe the author's relationship with the candidate
2.   Highlight the academic, professional, and personal strengths that the writer has personally observed
3.   Support every claim with an example or anecdote
4.   Compare the candidate to others in his/her peer group

Here are several recommendation letters for business school candidates with international work experience.   To protect the privacy of the writer and applicant, the names of all people, classes, schools, places, and companies have been changed.

Letter #30:   Student with International Educational Experience

As the Dean of Students in the Department of Finance at Shanghai University, I first met Sophia Wu during her freshman year.   I was immediately impressed by her intelligence and commitment to her work.   Shanghai University encourages academic success and self-motivation by waiving the tuition for students who distinguish themselves academically.   During her undergraduate program, Sophia earned a merit-based, full-tuition scholarship for all four years.   In both of my classes (Advanced Financial Theory and Options & Derivatives), Sophia earned a perfect 5 grade, which is equivalent to an A in the United States.   In 2008, she graduated in the top 1% of her class with a BA in International Relations and Finance.

As her professor, I was impressed by Sophia's determination to learn as much as possible about global finance.   She was a vibrant contributor to class discussions who offered intelligent and well-reasoned opinions on the topics at hand.   Despite her tremendous work load (full-time studies and a part-time job), Sophia frequently asked me to recommend additional reading material.   On several occasions, when the titles I suggested were not available on campus, I lent Sophia copies from my own personal library.   Within a few weeks, she included the new information in her research papers and class discussions.

One of Sophia's most astonishing strengths is her ability to speak five languages.   At one point, I noticed that she preferred to read in English, although it was not her native tongue.   When I asked her how she managed to learn the language so well, including intricate technical terms, I was amazed to discover that Sophia memorized articles from *The Economist, Wall Street Journal,* and *Investor's Business Daily* to familiarize herself with business terminology.   Sophia brought the same level of dedication to her coursework, never settling for anything less than full mastery of a theory or idea.

On one occasion, Sophia translated several chapters of various Financial Management and Economics textbooks that had been published in English, but not in Chinese or Cantonese.   She completed the translation quickly and accurately, which provided a better learning opportunity for the entire class. This incident demonstrates not only Sophia's impressive language skills, but her altruistic personality.   I admired her willingness to extend herself on behalf of her peers.

During the last year of her studies, Sophia volunteered for a research project for the Chinese government that investigated the potential long-term economic impact of the 2008 Olympic Games in Beijing.   Sophia conducted an extensive analysis of the costs and benefits of the construction of the Bird's Nest, which was a $50 million (USD) facility that was designed to house the games.   Her conclusions, which pointed out the long-term opportunities to use the venue for national sporting and entertainment events, were officially presented to the Chinese Olympic Planning Committee in 2006.   I have rarely seen a student deliver such insightful, high quality work.

In recognition of her exceptional academic performance, Sophia received a scholarship to attend a prestigious management course at Harvard University in 2007.   Only one award was given for this advanced seminar in Global Financial Management; Sophia competed with over 1,000 qualified applicants to attend the class. The course material, which was presented by professors from America, provided her with an exciting new perspective of the financial industry.   At the end of her third year of studies, Sophia received a coveted internship at the World Bank, where she prepared financial forecasts and performed analyses on their administrative and budgetary operations.   Sophia was one of only six students in the world to be awarded this opportunity, which provided invaluable experience in the field.

Based on Sophia's superior academic performance, I strongly encouraged her to pursue a graduate degree at Shanghai University; to defray her costs, we also offered her a position as a part-time Instructor.   However, Sophia had already received several job offers, including one from Venus Software Systems, where she had been working part-time for two years.   Excited by the growth possibilities in the technology industry, Sophia accepted the position as a Financial Analyst at Venus, where she was quickly promoted to Financial Director.   Sophia's diverse skills in finance and management enabled this small firm to gain a foothold in the global software market.

In the past few years, I have kept abreast of Sophia's impressive professional progress.   As expected, she has matured into a skilled analyst who has much to offer the financial industry.   As a professor, I have rarely encountered a student as intelligent, talented and tenacious as Sophia. I recommend her with the highest enthusiasm for whatever program she chooses to join.

Our Assessment: The author of this letter did an exceptional job of selling Sophia's analytical skills and flair for foreign languages.   By citing her numerous internships and seminars, which she attended on a competitive basis, the author convinced the committee that Sophia was a tenacious and talented young woman.

Letter #31:   Global Technology Experience

Please accept this letter as my enthusiastic endorsement of Ms. Bridget O'Donnell's application to business school. I have known Bridget since 2004, when she began the Master's degree program in Computer Science & Technology at Northwestern University.   During her two years on campus, I taught three of Bridget's software classes and served as her graduate thesis instructor.   As a result, I feel well qualified to assess her personal and intellectual strengths.

Before she enrolled at Northwestern, Bridget completed her Bachelor's degree in Computer Engineering at Cambridge University in London.   Consequently, she brought a keen understanding of international software issues to her graduate classes.   Bridget was a vibrant contributor in my three courses, including Advanced Systems Design, Software Theory and Application, and Marketing Research and Analysis.   She consistently asked perceptive questions about global software issues that her peers never considered.   The depth and quality of our discussions would have been significantly lower without Bridget's participation.

Under my direction, Bridget completed a master's thesis entitled, "Establishing a Market for Wireless Technology in an Unwired World," which earned significant praise in the industry.   For this complex project, Bridget evaluated the potential market for internet and cellular phone service in developing parts of India and Pakistan, where electricity has only recently arrived.   To complete her work, Bridget interviewed hundreds of executives, professors, and technical experts across the globe, including several who barely spoke English.   By listening carefully to each person's piece of the puzzle (and carefully digesting what she learned), Bridget made thoughtful recommendations that would allow existing companies to bring wireless services to a previously untapped market.   Her subsequent presentation won first prize at the Global Telecommunications Alliance Seminar, along with a $100,000 cash prize.   As her advisor, I was tremendously proud of the quality and impact of Bridget's research.

Throughout her graduate program, Bridget made a tangible contribution to research and analytical organizations on campus, including the Marketing Research and Analysis Club, the Center for Global Business Development, and the Graduate Student Technology Club.   Through these groups, Bridget shared her skills in computers and information technology with her professors and peers. As the President of the Graduate Student Technology Club, Bridget gave several presentations to undergraduate students, to help them transform their ideas into marketable consumer products.   She also served as a judge for the Undergraduate Business Plan Competition, which funded a number of promising entrepreneurial ventures. By setting clear priorities and managing her time effectively, Bridget achieved impressive results as a student, researcher, and leader.   She also gained an aptitude for critical reasoning and analysis that will serve her well in business school.

After completing her Master's degree in 2006, Bridget accepted a position as a Director of Technology at AT&T, which utilizes her significant background in computer science and engineering.   Not surprisingly, she has also become intrigued by the thought of launching her own venture in the technology industry.   In my long career as an educator, I have rarely met a student as mature and focused as Bridget.   She is also a woman of exemplary character who can train and motivate other people.   Bridget's superior communication skills, including her fluency in Spanish and Portuguese, will be a tremendous asset in a multinational program such as XXX.

Please contact me at phone number or at email address if you require additional information about Bridget.   I offer her my strongest recommendation.

Our Assessment: By the time she applied to business school, this candidate was a leader in her field with a number of publications and patents to her credit.   This recommendation letter offers a first-hand glimpse into Bridget's performance in graduate school, when she transformed a simple idea into a winning project and a lucrative career. Thanks to this author, the committee learned more about the depth and breadth of her contributions on campus during her years at Northwestern, where she helped other students achieve their professional dreams.

How long have you known the applicant and in what capacity?

I am pleased to offer a letter of reference for Janet Wu. I have known Janet since June of 2005, when she accepted a position as a Tax Analyst with the Bank of Tokyo-Mitsubishi in Hong Kong. I was Janet's co-worker and indirect manager for three years, in my role as Vice-President of International Taxation for several of the jurisdictions that she handles. As a graduate of XXXX Business School (1995), I am confident that Janet will be a great addition to your program.

What is the applicant's greatest strength? Please give an example.

Tax projects must be resolved in a short timeframe, which requires a rare combination of organization, conscientiousness and a scrupulous attention to detail. By consistently demonstrating these traits, Janet has assumed the responsibility for several high priority projects in seven Asian countries. With minimal guidance, she quickly became an insightful contributor to the group. On one occasion, after she familiarized herself with our reports and processes, Janet identified a way to streamline the system. By redesigning our annual tax package and other commonly used reports, she enabled the reader to easily pinpoint the information that he needed to make decisions.

One of Janet's most challenging projects was handling the bank's 2009 IRS audit, which required her to wade through several years' worth of data to make sense of the positions that were taken, including many cases with inadequate documentation. Janet was meticulous in her analysis; she researched multiple leads and responded thoughtfully to all questions that were asked. After handling such a difficult project with grace and flexibility, Janet was given increased responsibilities within the department.

Please describe the applicant's greatest accomplishment.

Within a few weeks of joining the bank, Janet reorganized several procedures that enabled our entire group to work more efficiently. She also used her skills in computer graphics to create and deliver concise presentations for senior managers. Our decision to promote her to a managerial position in 2007, although she did not possess the mandatory ten years experience, was extremely unorthodox for this department. We have never regretted making an exception for Janet, whose performance has continually exceeded our expectations.

In the Tax Department, responsibilities are assigned with great deliberation because of the highly sensitive nature of the work. Janet has proven herself to be a woman of exceptional competence and integrity, handling tax matters for several significant foreign jurisdictions. Without exception, Janet handled these important functions with the competence and discretion one would expect of a far more seasoned professional.

In what area does the applicant need improvement?

Janet's only weakness is her tendency to expect too much from herself in comparison to her more seasoned colleagues. Fortunately, rather than become discouraged, she continually seeks opportunities to learn. On several occasions, Janet has asked me to recommend books that would enable her to better understand a topic or problem. On her own time, she visits our tax library to study accounting, tax and legal concepts, which enable her to contribute to group discussions.

Because the Bank of Tokyo-Mitsubishi was Janet's first post-collegiate job, she was unfamiliar with the bureaucratic processes of a non-academic environment. Once she adapted to our corporate culture, she learned how to take command of her situation and find viable ways to promote change. By championing small projects that have a large impact, Janet has gained a reputation for being proactive and politically savvy in our large organization.

Is there anything else we should know about the applicant?

Janet also has an impressive command of foreign languages. In addition to her fluency in English, Mandarin and Taiwanese, she has also taken the initiative to read and write Hindi. Our overseas contacts have consistently praised Janet for her preparation, efficiency and willingness to "speak their language." Before she came to the bank, many of these countries failed to send their information to her predecessor in a timely manner. Now, they respond with diligence and enthusiasm. I credit Janet for cultivating such a strong rapport with her colleagues.

Few people in my career have impressed me as positively as Janet Wu. In her five years at the bank, she has improved the efficiency of her department and has earned the respect of her clients and peers.   I recommend Janet without reservation.   Please contact me at (phone number) or (email address) if you require additional information.

<u>Our Assessment</u>:   The author of this letter is a well-known banking professional who rarely writes such positive recommendations.   Consequently, his glowing endorsement of Janet to his alma mater made a quite an impression on the admissions committee.   Once again, the strength is in the details; this is a great letter filled with concrete examples of Janet's strengths.   Her international background and language fluencies were particularly well-perceived in the admissions process.

Chapter 13:   Letters that Explain a Gap on a Candidate's Resume

Some candidates, for various personal or professional reasons, have a gap on their resume of more than six months. In these situations, it is incredibly helpful if an objective third-party can document the candidate's activities during this "missing" period of time.   Ideally, the author should be honest, but put the best possible "spin" on the gap.

If a candidate has taken time off due to illness or injury – or to take care of small children or elderly parents – there is no need to "justify" or embellish the decision.   The committee understands that there are personal and family emergencies that take priority in people's lives.

However, if a candidate has been unemployed for an extended period of time – and was not busy with family responsibilities – the committee WILL expect that person to use his/her time in a constructive manner by volunteering, tutoring, or trying to launch a business.   These are all admirable activities that can enhance a candidate's application, if they are documented by a well-written recommendation letter.

The letter should adhere to the same principles we have reiterated throughout this publication.   It should:

1.   Describe the author's relationship with the candidate
2.   Highlight the academic, professional, and personal strengths that the writer has personally observed
3.   Support every claim with an example or anecdote
4.   Compare the candidate to others in his/her peer group

Here are several recommendation letters for business school candidates who had a gap on their resume.   To protect the privacy of the writer and applicant, the names of all people, classes, schools, places, and companies have been changed.

Letter #33:   Explains Time Off from Work or School

As her faculty advisor at Brigham Young University, I quickly discovered that Adrienne Shaw was an intelligent young woman with great ambition and an engaging personality.   Her impressive achievements in the classroom made her a popular and respected student on campus.   Yet few of her peers or faculty members know of the struggle that Adrienne has endured during the last two years, which have made her a stronger person with a passion to help others.

With little advance warning, her younger brother died of AIDS in early 2008.   Although Adrienne's family had known of his diagnosis, they were emotionally unprepared for his death.   At first, Adrienne accepted the news stoically and refused to acknowledge her own grief.   She opted to keep the news private, rather than share it with the Brigham Young community.   As the lone faculty member to know the circumstances of Chad's death, I was simultaneously honored and shaken.   Although I treasured the trust that Adrienne had placed in me, I questioned whether I could provide adequate support to her during such a devastating time.

Amazingly, Adrienne completed the spring semester with a 3.8 GPA and promised to return in the fall.   Over the summer, however, she decided to delay her return for a full year in order to process her grief.   Adrienne's motivation was anything but self-indulgent; within a month of Chad's death, she joined a program at her local hospice designed to promote AIDS awareness in the community.   During her year off from Brigham Young, Adrienne presented over one hundred seminars on AIDS prevention to local schools, women's groups, and clinics in Salt Lake City.

Upon her return to Brigham Young in the fall of 2009, Adrienne continued to teach classes and train new participants in the AIDS awareness program.   During the past year, she has been a visible advocate for AIDS prevention in Salt Lake City.   To my delight, Adrienne's year off gave her an increased appreciation of life and its wondrous opportunities.   In that spirit, she has re-directed her professional goals to an entirely new area.   Before her brother's death, Adrienne was on track for a career in marketing and advertising.   After her return to Brigham Young, she committed herself to a career in public service.

During her absence from campus, Adrienne became well acquainted with several AIDS advocates in Salt Lake City. She was horrified by the shabby treatment that many patients received, either because of insurance restrictions or the stigma of their illness.   She is committed to fighting their cause.   In many ways, her commitment is a way to honor Chad's legacy, to provide a voice for patients whose needs are not being met.   I have no doubt that Adrienne will tackle business school with the same style and grace that she brings to everything else she does.

As you peruse Adrienne's MBA application, you will see her grades and GMAT scores, her numerous awards and accolades, but nothing about her greatest accomplishment of all; she transformed a devastating loss into a way to help others. I desperately wanted to relate this episode, because it characterizes what this remarkable young woman is all about.

With her unique personal strengths, Adrienne is destined to achieve great things.   Grab her while you can!

Our Assessment: This letter captures the human aspects of the candidate in a highly articulate way.   In addition to documenting Adrienne's academic record, the letter also provides a valid explanation for her time off from school. By discussing Adrienne's volunteer work on behalf of AIDS, the author conveyed the young woman's exemplary character and dedication.   The committee had a greater understanding of who Adrienne was and what she hoped to accomplish in the future.

Letter #34: Explains Time Off from Work or School

I am proud to recommend Vivian Greer for admission to XXX Business School. Vivian is a highly intelligent and perceptive young woman who came to Cornell to study clinical depression in rural women and children. The project was an extension of her previous research at the Shanghai University, where she published the landmark 1999 paper on the actual vs. published rates of clinical depression in children. Although many European universities subsequently offered her graduate support, Vivian chose Cornell because of our close proximity to the Rockefeller Research Institute in New York City. We were honored to admit Vivian, as she brought compelling credentials as a scholar to our institution.

We initially expected Vivian to join our program in September of 2001, but her plans were unexpectedly altered by the 9/11 terrorist attacks. With no advance warning, the US State Department declined to issue student visas to candidates from 96 countries, including China. To our horror, Vivian's paperwork was tied up for nearly a year until the US government implemented the appropriate security regulations for student visas. During that time, we held Vivian's position open, as she was our first choice to receive the Carol Young Memorial Fellowship. After the travel ban was lifted, we were delighted to finally have Vivian on our campus for the Fall, 2002 semester.

In just two years, Vivian completed an impressive national study on the occurrence of clinical depression in rural areas. On several occasions, she worked with local women's and children's groups to develop and implement effective educational programs in local schools. When asked, Vivian traveled at her own expense to give lectures and training seminars to willing participants. I was amazed by the amount and quality of data that Vivian amassed in such a short period of time.

Vivian will graduate this spring with a doctoral degree in Clinical Psychology. She has a perfect 4.0 grade point average, although she consistently took the most demanding courses. During her time at Cornell, Vivian has published six articles in peer-reviewed journals and is completing three other manuscripts for future review. She has presented her work at four national seminars, including the prestigious National Psychological Symposium, which honored her as their 2006 Researcher of the Year. Vivian is, without question, the most dynamic and successful researcher I have worked with in my forty-year career.

During her time at our institution, Vivian has also demonstrated her skills as an advocate and publicist. In conjunction with her work on mental health education, she wrote the text for several book chapters, along with informational brochures for parents, alumni, and potential donors. Thanks to Vivian's eloquence, she has received numerous financial contributions and interview requests from the media. Despite her obvious potential for personal promotion, Vivian prefers to keep the focus on our work. When praised, she is quick to credit the entire team for their contribution.

Vivian is consistent, enthusiastic, and a pleasure to work with. I highly recommend her for XXX Business School, where she can spread her excitement for mental health education throughout the campus community. Thank you for the opportunity to recommend such a special and impressive young woman.

Our Assessment: This letter was written by a distinguished professor with an international reputation for his research on depression. His willingness to endorse Vivian's candidacy with such enthusiasm was a testament to her character and skills.

Letter #35:   Explains Time Off from Work or School

How long have you known the applicant and in what capacity?

I have known Rebecca Stone for six years as a volunteer and friend.   For the past three years, we have served as Co-Presidents of the Miami chapter of Aphrodite & Company, which offers free services and educational programs for cancer patients, survivors and their families.   Rebecca's talents as a manager and fundraiser have dramatically enhanced our success at all levels of the organization.   I have no doubt that she will be an exceptional leader following her graduation from business school.

What is the applicant's greatest strength?   Please give an example.

Rebecca's greatest talent is fundraising on behalf of cancer research.   Like many volunteers, her inspiration comes directly from the heart.   As a child, she lost her mother to ovarian cancer when she was just thirty-six years old. After Rebecca worked through her grief, she became determined to learn as much as possible about cancer. Ultimately, she opted to pursue a career as a public health advocate in the Miami community.

Please describe the applicant's greatest accomplishment.

Between 2005 and 2008, Rebecca raised over $6 million for the Miami chapter of Aphrodite & Company, which funded an additional wing of our Main Street facility.   As a result, we can now offer free respite services for the caregivers who are enrolled in our hospice program.   Rebecca also negotiated a reduced contracting fee for our Main Street renovation, which created three rooms for out-of-town guests who cannot afford to pay for lodging. Without Rebecca's aggressive fundraising efforts, these improvements would not have been possible.

In late 2007, Rebecca organized a gala benefit on behalf of Miami Oncology Associates, which offers free and reduced price services for indigent patients.   She also volunteers at the center, where she draws blood, conducts lab tests and provides emotional support to chemotherapy patients.   Thanks to her early experiences as a caregiver, Rebecca understands the challenges that patients endure on their uneasy road to recovery.   She is a kind and compassionate friend to all who enter our doors.

In what area does the applicant need improvement?

Rebecca's only area for improvement is learning to say "no" to requests when she is too busy to handle them.   Many times, she is besieged by requests for money, time, and support from individual clients and organizations.   Rebecca is also a popular speaker in the community.   Rather than decline a request for help, she will work herself ragged trying to accommodate everyone and everything.   In the end, Rebecca would benefit from taking a step back and passing these tasks on to someone else.

Is there anything else we should know about the applicant?

In early 2008, Rebecca faced a formidable challenge when she was diagnosed with breast cancer.   After our initial shock, we feared that the disease might diminish her ability to work for our group.   Thankfully, Rebecca's illness enhanced her commitment as a volunteer; she returned to Aphrodite & Company after a one-year leave of absence with two profound revelations; (1) that breast cancer awareness must be a cornerstone of our services, and (2) that she wanted to form a non-profit organization to champion women's health care issues.

Rebecca is particularly committed to helping patients who do not have health insurance.   In her role as a public health advocate, she has repeatedly lobbied Congress about the alarming statistics concerning uninsured women, who are significantly more likely to have non-diagnosed cases of breast, lung, colon, uterine, and ovarian cancer. Within her lifetime, Rebecca hopes to champion a more compassionate health care system, in which the needs of the patients are a higher priority than the financial compensation of the providers.   After seeing her in action, I am confident that Rebecca will succeed.   From my experience, Rebecca is the smartest, kindest, most determined woman I know.   She is truly the best that our community has to offer.

Our Assessment: This letter documents Rebecca's impressive ability to survive a tragedy and find meaning in her pain.   The committee was deeply moved by her personal story, along with her continual commitment to help other women who suffer from the same disease.   Additionally, Rebecca's work as a community advocate was a great fit for the program in which she eventually enrolled.

Chapter 14: Letters that Document an Adversity in the Candidate's Life

Some candidates face formidable obstacles to graduate from college and apply to business school.   Due to personal events beyond their control, such as illness, language deficiencies, learning disabilities, or cultural barriers, even basic milestones are difficult to achieve.   Nevertheless, these extraordinary candidates are top performers in the classroom and work environment because of their insatiable dedication and tenacity - they have a level of focus, maturity, and resilience that sets them apart from the crowd.

Many times, candidates will discuss these obstacles in their application essays, both to share their background with the committee and to document their problems with the GMAT.   Unfortunately, in a large applicant pool, it is often difficult to distinguish genuine hardships from ordinary excuses.   From our experience, the information will carry *far* more weight if it is confirmed in a recommendation letter from an objective third party who has no vested interest in the admissions decision.

Although these issues are private – and deeply difficult to talk about – the way a candidate deals with them is an indication of his/her character.   If you have the applicant's permission to mention the issue – and you are willing to do so – you can provide the committee with insight into the candidate's life that they never could have acquired any other way.

The letter should adhere to the same principles we have reiterated throughout this publication.   It should:

1. Describe the author's relationship with the candidate
2. Highlight the academic, professional, and personal strengths that the writer has personally observed
3. Support every claim with an example or anecdote
4. Compare the candidate to others in his/her peer group

Here are several recommendation letters for business school candidates who have survived an obstacle or setback. To protect the privacy of the writer and applicant, the names of all people, classes, schools, places, and companies have been changed.

Letter #36:   Overcoming an Obstacle (Dual JD/MBA Program)

I am pleased to write a letter of recommendation on behalf of Ms. Joanne Rogers, who has applied for admission to the JD/MBA program at Northwestern University.   I have known Joanne since September of 2006, when she enrolled in my course entitled Advanced Oncology: Theory and Practice at Stanford Medical School.   Based on her superlative performance, I am confident that Joanne has the requisite intelligence and drive to succeed in a rigorous JD/MBA program.

From our first class meeting, Joanne demonstrated her superior intelligence and work ethic.   She followed my lectures closely and asked insightful questions about the material.   When I assigned outside reading, Joanne immediately completed the assignments and discussed their relevance in class.   By doing so, she revealed her outstanding command of cellular biology, on both a theoretical and practical basis.

On several occasions, Joanne attended my review sessions to ensure that she understood the material - it is, after all, one of the toughest courses in the entire MD program.   Joanne was one of the few students who received an A in the class, after earning nearly perfect scores on all of her exams.   Based on her interest and competence, I suggested that Joanne tutor another student who was struggling in the course.   With her nurturing personality and impressive command of the material, I couldn't imagine anyone better suited to help him.

In my long career, I have rarely taken the time to write a recommendation on behalf of a student.   Joanne is that rare exception.   Her performance in the MD program at Stanford is particularly noteworthy, because she is an Army veteran who lost both of her legs during a combat mission in Desert Storm.   Rest assured, although Ms. Rogers cannot walk, and is in fact confined to a wheelchair, she refuses to identify herself as disabled.   Instead, she focuses strictly on what she *can* do, which is nothing short of amazing.

Joanne is an excellent student, a compassionate clinician, and a seasoned researcher who has won several awards and published numerous papers in peer-reviewed journals.   Joanne is also an insightful physician-scientist with a continual passion to learn more, know more, and do more.   As a result, she is a valuable asset to whatever project she joins.

Based on my interactions with her, I am confident that Joanne will excel in all aspects of the JD/MBA program.   With her rare combination of personal and professional attributes – including her unparalleled motivation - she will undoubtedly succeed at whatever she decides to do.

I offer Joanne my strongest recommendation.   Please contact me at XXX-XXX-XXXX or at email address if you would like additional information.

<u>Our Assessment</u>:   This author is a distinguished physician who rarely writes letters of recommendation.   His willingness to endorse Joanne was a testament to her character and achievements.   Most impressively, this author did not make the candidate's physical limitations the focus of the letter – or use them as an excuse for anything.   Instead, he focused on her strengths - and what she *could* do – which made an indelible impression on the committee.

Letter #37:   Overcoming an Obstacle

I have known Mrs. Amy Lee for three years in my role as Associate Professor of Psychology at the University of Virginia.   During this time, Amy has completed considerable work under my direction, including two courses in Abnormal Psychology, a three-credit Research Practicum and her Senior Thesis.   Amy has also served as my Research Assistant for a project on women's health.   As a student and researcher, Amy has consistently demonstrated the following strengths:

1. Academic Excellence.   My advanced courses in Abnormal Psychology require considerable reading in various textbooks and peer-reviewed journals; they also require students to write a comprehensive term paper that goes beyond the scope of the source material.   Both semesters, Amy displayed a remarkable ability to stay abreast of the assignments and comprehend the subtle details of each article.   In class, Amy discussed the reading intelligently and related the information back to earlier topics. She was unquestionably one of the brightest students in the class.

2. Research Skills.   During her Research Practicum, Amy completed an impressive literature review that investigated the barriers to health care delivery in minority populations.   To do so, she analyzed dozens of relevant studies and presented the essential details of each one in her final report.   Later, for her Senior Thesis, Amy conducted individual research on the availability of health care in an inner city neighborhood in Richmond.   Her paper was one of the best I have ever seen.

Based on her exemplary performance, I selected Amy as my Research Assistant for a National Institutes of Health project to improve the delivery of prenatal care for minority women.   As part of this endeavor, Amy collaborated with professors and physicians from twelve other U.S. colleges and universities.   Thus far, the quality of her work has been excellent; our preliminary results will soon be published in *Lancet*.

3. Time Management.   Amy's achievements are particularly impressive, considering the competing demands on her time.   When she began her second semester of Abnormal Psychology, Amy had just given birth to her first child. Nevertheless, she attended every class and completed all of her work in an exemplary manner, without any delays or excuses.   During her Research Practicum, Amy was taking care of her son, going to school full-time, and collecting data at several local women's clinics.   She somehow kept up this incredible pace for an entire year, without complaining or falling behind.   As her professor and supervisor, I was deeply impressed by Amy's ability to conduct quality research and maintain an outstanding performance in her classes, in addition to her many responsibilities at home.   I have rarely met anyone with comparable organizational and planning skills.

4. Compassion & Perseverance.   Throughout her life, Amy has displayed an uncommon level of grace and perseverance.   At age six, she lost both of her parents in an auto accident in Korea.   Later, after years in an orphanage, Amy faced the daunting challenge of adapting to life in the U.S., where her adoptive parents moved. Thankfully, Amy was an excellent student who quickly became fluent in English.   She has also been extremely loving and loyal to her adoptive parents.   In the spring of 2008, Amy made an extraordinary gesture when she became the primary caregiver for her mother, who was battling terminal cancer.   Despite the many complications in her life, including her full-time course load and the care of a newborn, Amy provided compassionate care during her mother's final days.   I applaud her willingness to open her heart and home in such a generous manner.

As one of the few Asian students at the University of Virginia, Amy has represented our school at numerous events, including the annual Asian-American Cultural Fair in Washington, DC.   She also promotes the University to prospective students in her native Korea, who might not otherwise consider a college in Virginia.   Because of her unique combination of strengths, including her kind and gracious personality, Amy has become a respected role model in the Asian-American community.

5. Weakness.   Amy's only weakness is her tendency to take on too much, which does not leave her with adequate time for rest and relaxation.   When she has a spare moment, Amy tends to take care of others, rather than herself. In the long run, I think she would benefit by striking a better balance between work and play.

Summary.   Amy is a remarkable woman who will be an asset to any program she decides to join.   I offer her my enthusiastic support.

Our Assessment: This letter documented the candidate's exceptional performance as a student and researcher. More importantly, it also confirmed her ability to balance these responsibilities with the demands of caring for a newborn child and an elderly parent.   After reading it, the committee realized what a motivated and effective person Amy was.

Letter #38:   Candidate with Learning Disabilities

How long have you known the applicant and in what capacity?

I am honored to write a reference letter on behalf of Damian Medeiros.   As an Associate Professor of History at Northeastern University, I taught Damian in three classes before I became his senior thesis advisor.   In this capacity, I spent the better part of an academic year working closely with him on a project that revealed his phenomenal strengths as a writer and investigator.

In our first class together, "The History of Gender Roles in America," Damian wrote with extraordinary insight on a number of exam topics.   In the summer of 2007, I was sufficiently impressed to hire Damian as a Research Assistant for a project that investigated the evolution of women's suffrage in America.   Damian did a superb job of collecting and analyzing materials for me, including several unpublished legislative reports from the 1890's, which suggested that New Hampshire residents were actually quite progressive on various women's issues.   To follow this intriguing lead, Damian decided to write his senior thesis on the suffrage movement in New England. In hindsight, I cannot remember another student being willing to tackle something even remotely as difficult and ambitious.

What is the applicant's greatest strength?   Please give an example.

As soon as he began his work, Damian encountered an unexpected obstacle; the New Hampshire Historical Society refused to release the documents he needed to complete his study.   Although most decisions of this nature are non-negotiable, Damian refused to give up.   Employing a rare combination of diligence and diplomacy, he petitioned the Society to release the documents that he needed for his work.   In a persuasive letter, Damian explained the historical value of the research and the new light that it would shed on a misunderstood period of American history. He also explained his particular interest in the topic, drawing parallels between the evolution of women's rights in Massachusetts and in his native Panama.   By taking a sincere and passionate approach, Damian convinced Dr. Emily Harris, the Director of the Society, to release the documents and discuss their relevance with him.

Please describe the applicant's greatest accomplishment.

Damian's undergraduate thesis was the best I have ever seen.   Although he was working in an unexplored area, he made convincing conjectures about the motives of the legislators and their subsequent efforts to promote gender equality in New Hampshire.   His thesis was also highly ambitious, requiring a large amount of original research and an ability to create an accurate picture of history from conflicting pieces of data.   From my perspective, Damian's writing was better than that of most graduate students I supervise.   Most impressively, Damian did not allow his own biases or expectations to cloud his judgment.   This skill will inevitably serve him well in business school.

In what area does the applicant need improvement?

Damian's only weakness is a disappointing GMAT score, which is a consequence of his lifelong struggle with learning disabilities.   Twenty years ago, Damian was diagnosed with dyslexia and ADHD, which impair his ability to do well on standardized tests.   Rather than request special accommodations for the GMAT, Damian took it under standard conditions.   In fact, for philosophical reasons, he has never requested special accommodations for any of his classes at Northeastern. As his professor, I respect Damian's decision to keep the focus on his talents, rather than his limitations.   By doing so, he has proven that he can perform at parity with other candidates under extremely stressful circumstances.   What more can you ask from a candidate?

Is there anything else we should know about the applicant?

Damian is not just an exceptional student, but a kind, generous, and hardworking young man.   Our department is infinitely richer for his having worked in it.   I recommend Damian without reservation for your program.

Our Assessment: This letter was written by a well-known professor at Northeastern who rarely writes such glowing letters of recommendation.   Automatically, the committee knew that this young man must be something special. The letter's strength is that the author knows the applicant well and is favorably impressed by his work.   The writer did a great job of citing specific examples of Damian's diligence and research skills.   By mentioning the learning disabilities at the END of the letter, he kept the focus on what the candidate could do, rather than on his deficiencies. By doing so, he distinguished Damian from the hundreds of other applicants with disappointing GMAT scores.

Chapter 15: Letters that Explain Low Grades or GMAT Scores

Many times, as part of their applications, candidates will attach a separate addendum to explain a disappointing grade or GMAT score. Their hope is that the explanation will somehow compensate for a less than stellar "number" on their application. Unfortunately, at highly competitive schools, these addendums rarely make a positive impact on the admissions committee.

Why? Most explanations are convoluted and self-serving – and difficult to verify. Other times, the excuse raises more questions than it actually answers, such as an announcement that the candidate does not perform well on standardized tests. Well, business school *requires* candidates to pass dozens of timed tests in a highly competitive environment; if you cannot handle a standardized test, how do you plan to complete the program? (I've yet to hear a persuasive answer to that question.)

If you have a disappointing grade or GMAT score – and a legitimate explanation for it – it is FAR better to have an objective third party document it in a persuasive recommendation letter. What are legitimate explanations?

- Medical emergencies that can be documented by a physician's letter
- A serious illness or death in the immediate family
- Military commitments
- Work commitments necessitated by financial emergencies
- Your native language is not English
- You have a documented learning disability, but did not request special accommodations for the GMAT

In these cases, a well-written letter that informs the committee of the situation (without making excuses for the candidate) can greatly enhance the application. The letter should adhere to the same principles we have reiterated throughout this publication. It should:

1. Describe the author's relationship with the candidate
2. Highlight the academic, professional, and personal strengths that the writer has personally observed
3. Support every claim with an example or anecdote
4. Compare the candidate to others in his/her peer group

Here are several recommendation letters for business school candidates with disappointing grades or GMAT scores. To protect the privacy of the writer and applicant, the names of all people, classes, schools, places, and companies have been changed.

Letter #39:   Explains Poor GMAT Scores / Military Commitment

I am pleased to write a letter of reference to support Wayne Carson's application to business school.   I have known Wayne for nearly seven years in my position as the President of the Greater Southwestern Mortgage Corporation in Phoenix, Arizona.   Since early 2004, Wayne has worked as an Appraisal Specialist under my supervision.

Professional Experience.   Before he came to work with us, Wayne obtained his Real Estate Sales License, Broker's License, and Appraisal Trainee License and worked as an appraiser for a competitive firm.   During the height of the refinancing boom in 2005, Wayne worked over 60 hours per week, in addition to managing his own personal portfolio of investment properties.   Impressed by his solid work ethic and knowledge of the industry, I was eager to have Wayne on board.

Professional Strengths.   As an Appraisal Specialist, Wayne works with our Asset Management Division on real estate transactions in twelve southwestern states. As a result, Wayne has an excellent command of the factors that affect a property's value in the commercial and residential markets.   Despite the volume and complexity of the work, Wayne excels at all aspects of selling, managing, and maintaining bank foreclosure properties.   He also reviews files for the REO department to help sell any bad loans or properties on the books.   By establishing fair market values for the properties, Wayne helps our sales departments sell our loans quickly, which improves our cash flow.

Interpersonal Strengths.   Like many industries, the real estate business is primarily about people.   Those who succeed do so by providing impeccable service that caters to their clients' needs.   With his amiable personality, Wayne excels at the interpersonal aspects of this business.   In any given situation, he displays a gracious confidence that immediately puts people at ease.   Wayne also works diligently to support the needs of his peers. During peak periods, he often works sixteen hour days, along with long shifts over the weekends.   Regardless of his competing priorities, Wayne is always willing to do his fair share of the work.

Motivation & Initiative.   Wayne is extremely motivated to learn more about the industry, both through formal classes and discussions with his peers.   In the fall of 2007, Wayne upgraded his skills by receiving his Residential Appraisers License and Certified Residential License.   Amazingly, he scored in the top 1% of all professionals on both exams, which earned him a Golden Appraisal Award, which is the most distinguished honor in the industry.

Military Commitment.   Although Wayne is clearly a talented professional, his most impressive commitment is to our country.   Since 2005, in addition to his real estate career, he has also been a soldier in the US Army Reserves.   In August of 2008, with virtually no notice, Wayne left the comfort of his home to complete a one-year stint in Iraq. Needless to say, we missed him terribly in the office and were delighted by his safe return. Unfortunately, Wayne's unexpected deployment had a negative effect on his ability to prepare for the GMAT.   After working with him for many years, I can confirm that Wayne's disappointing score on the exam is by no means indicative of his ability to succeed in business.   He took the test in September of 2009, just three days after he returned from Iraq.   Under those circumstances, I am amazed that he did as well as he did.

Summary.   In my 30-year career in real estate, I have worked with hundreds of brokers, loan officers and attorneys who wanted to build their own successful real estate businesses.   I would easily rank Wayne in the top 1% of that group.   I am particularly impressed by Wayne's willingness to defer his professional career in favor of attending graduate school.   He has repeatedly turned down my offer of a promotion to focus his energy on obtaining his MBA. With his entrepreneurial flair, I am certain that he will add a unique perspective to the student community.   Please contact me at email address if you would like to further discuss Wayne's application.

Our Assessment: In addition to documenting Wayne's impeccable work history, this letter also provides a valid explanation for his disappointing GMAT scores.   Although Wayne discussed these issues in his essays, his credibility was enhanced by third-party corroboration of the events in question.

Letter #40:   Explains Low Grades from a Foreign University

I am the Dean of Students at the Universidad de Costa Rica in San Pedro, which is one of the largest and most prestigious universities in the nation.   Between 2005 and 2009, Mr. Lorenzo Ruiz was one of our most diligent and successful undergraduate students.   Among his many achievements, Mr. Ruiz:

- Completed a dual major in Chemistry and Applied Mathematics in just four years

- Consistently scored in the top 1% of his class, which included the best science students in the nation

- Won merit scholarships that totaled $50,000 USD from DuPont Chemical and Ciba-Geigy

- Served as Class President his senior year and delivered the keynote speech at his commencement exercise

- Published three research papers in the *Journal of the International Chemical Society*

- Completed a prestigious internship at DuPont Chemical in the U.S. (2008), which led to a full-time job offer (and sponsorship for visa)

- Demonstrated written and oral fluency in English, Spanish and Portuguese

As Mr. Ruiz's research advisor, I was deeply impressed by his intelligence and work ethic.   For his degree, he investigated the use of biodegradable pesticides for fruits and vegetables, which will prevent insect infestation without leaving a residue or contaminating the water supply.   Initially, Mr. Ruiz faced several obstacles to achieve his seemingly incompatible objectives.   Nevertheless, he remained dedicated to his work.   Eventually, he developed a promising prototype that DuPont Chemical is interested in patenting.

Mr. Ruiz has consistently demonstrated that he is an intelligent, driven, and perceptive scientist.   He was also one of the best students and researchers I have ever taught.   Recently, when he requested this letter, Mr. Ruiz asked me to document the difference in grading between the two university systems.   Unlike schools in the U.S., the Universidad de Costa Rica does not convert students' grades to a percentage or letter scale.   We simply report the raw numbers. To put the information into perspective – and to compare individual applicants – the committee should note the "Class Ranking" at the bottom of the final page of the transcript, which reveals how Mr. Ruiz's grades compared to those of his classmates - he ranked 3rd out of 1,450 students.   By all measurable criteria, Mr. Ruiz was one of our most successful and accomplished undergraduates.

Based on Mr. Ruiz's success at our school, followed by his professional experience at DuPont Chemical, I am confident that he will compete successfully at a U.S. business school.   I offer him my strongest recommendation. Please contact me if you have any questions about Mr. Ruiz's academic records.   I will be happy to clarify any concerns you may have.

Our Assessment: Students from foreign universities face an additional hurdle in the admissions process.   Many times, the committee is not familiar with the institution where the candidate completed his/her undergraduate studies. Other times, the grading system is different than that in the U.S., which makes it difficult to "translate" grades from one system to another.

In this case, the student was wise enough to ask the Dean of Students at his undergraduate school to explain their policy of presenting "raw" or unscaled grades on their students' transcripts; the only way to learn the "full story" about a candidate's academic performance was to view the Class Ranking.   Thankfully, this candidate also obtained a top score on the GMAT, which eliminated any concern the committee had about his ability to succeed.

Letter #41:   Explains Poor Grades & Language Deficiency

How long have you known the applicant and in what capacity?

I am writing this letter to give my highest possible recommendation for Mr. Sandeep Patel.   In 2007, I hired Sandeep as a junior software developer at my new company, Incandescent Software Solutions.   At first, I was hesitant to hire a college student with limited experience, but Sandeep won me over with his confidence and enthusiasm.   I have never regretted taking a chance on him.   Since 2007, Sandeep has participated in every aspect of the business, from core product development to marketing and sales.   In hindsight, his entrepreneurial abilities proved to be exceptionally helpful in growing my business.

What is the applicant's greatest strength?   Please give an example.

With minimal guidance, Sandeep developed my company's initial software product, which provided free shopping cart and checkout services to online vendors who sold their products on eBay.   His programming was of excellent quality, which belied his lack of experience.   I was most impressed by Sandeep's willingness to exceed my expectations, which were admittedly quite high.   As I struggled with the challenges of my startup venture, I gave Sandeep an extremely demanding work load and I had little tolerance for mistakes.   Fortunately, Sandeep was smart, fast, and motivated.   On the rare occasion that he made an error, he quickly corrected it and learned from the experience.

Please describe the applicant's greatest accomplishment.

In addition to his work as a programmer, Sandeep also designed the advertising materials that we used to market the product, including a web site that accepted direct sales.   After launching the web site, Sandeep set up new client accounts over the phone and resolved numerous technical issues.   To my surprise, Sandeep's technical and interpersonal skills proved to be an excellent sales tool.   By promoting various enhancements and upgrades to our customers, he generated $825,000 in incremental sales.   Considering the novelty of the product and our limited presence in the market, this was a remarkable achievement.

In what area does the applicant need improvement?

Sandeep's sales and presentation skills are particularly impressive because he did not grow up speaking English. When he arrived in the U.S. in 2005, Sandeep had only a cursory knowledge of the language.   Although he struggled academically because of this deficiency, Sandeep never lost sight of his goals.   Throughout the time I have known him, he has worked diligently to perfect his fluency, both through college classes and on-the-job experience.   Even now, Sandeep carries a pocket notebook with him at all times to write down difficult words and phrases.   By anyone's estimation, he has certainly succeeded.   Most of our clients would be stunned to learn that Sandeep is not a native speaker of English.

Is there anything else we should know about the applicant?

Sandeep also showed tremendous poise and maturity when faced with personal setbacks. During his first year with our firm, his younger sister died from leukemia just weeks after she arrived for treatment in the US.   Sandeep struggled with profound sadness as he recovered from this unexpected loss. Fortunately, he remained committed to his work and became an inspiring example for those who struggle with clinical depression.   Regardless of his troubles, Sandeep's performance at work was always exceptional.   I was profoundly moved by the maturity and elegance he demonstrated at such a young age.

Thanks to Sandeep's success at Incandescent Software Solutions, I recently promoted him to Director of Information Technology.   In my 30 years of managing IT professionals, including 5 years in an entrepreneurial capacity, I have never seen anyone as motivated as Sandeep.   With his impressive technical and interpersonal skills, along with his ambition to succeed, there is no limit to what this talented young man will accomplish.

<u>Our Assessment</u>:   This letter provides a detailed explanation of Sandeep's ability to seize an opportunity and make the most of it. His skills in sales and marketing, along with his managerial strengths, allowed him to advance to a senior technical position in a short period of time. The committee was particularly impressed by his ability to master a new language without formal classes. His initiative and maturity were well-perceived in the admissions process.

Chapter 16:   Hall of Shame: References That Do NOT Open Doors

Throughout this book, we have offered numerous examples of terrific recommendation letters.   From an admissions perspective, our discussion would not be complete unless we included a few samples of bad letters that failed to enhance the candidates' applications.   Sad to say, but the letters in this chapter are typical of what we see for many business school candidates.   How do applicants wind up with such lackluster references?   Three possibilities come to mind:

1.   The author did not know what to say, so (s)he said as little as possible.

2.   The author was not particularly enthusiastic about the candidate, but did not decline his/her request for a letter.

3.   The author blatantly sabotaged the candidate, for any number of reasons.

By publishing these bad letters, we hope to demonstrate the difference between a great reference letter and a mediocre one.   In the admissions game, it can make the difference between acceptance and rejection.

For applicants, this chapter is compelling evidence of why you should choose your writers carefully and give them as much supporting documentation as possible.   For writers, these letters are a convenient yardstick for you to use when you are asked to write a letter of recommendation.   As a general rule, if you cannot be any more enthusiastic about a candidate than the authors of the letters in this chapter, you should decline the applicant's request for a letter. You are NOT helping the candidate if you are ambiguous, ambivalent, or unwilling to provide sufficient details.

Letter #42:   Ambiguous Letter

Who is Helen Resnick?   A high-energy young woman with a keen eye on the future. She is also a person of tremendous intelligence who has a gift for working with computers.

Helen has matured greatly over the last few years.   Initially, her lack of commitment to her studies stood in the way of her personal and academic growth.   Thankfully, at the end of her junior year, I witnessed a dramatic shift in Helen's ability to focus.   For the first time, she was able to produce a consistently high quality of work in all of her classes.   In fact, Helen's skills in science and technology bolstered her confidence and inspired her to work harder in other areas.

In 2009, Helen started her own web design company.   After researching what was required to launch a new business, she marketed her services to corporate clients in Boston.   As she became more empowered, Helen became excited by the many technical courses available to her.

As an emerging computer scientist, Helen has taught herself numerous computer languages and has taken distance-learning classes through the local technology institute.   Helen's career plan is to combine her love of technology law with her desire to run her own business.   After completing her business degree, Helen hopes to develop her entrepreneurial skills by opening her own technology firm.

The faculty at the University of Massachusetts believes that Helen's growth over the last twelve months has been nothing short of remarkable.   Her focus and patience have enabled her to make friends; as her confidence grew, she began to contribute to class discussions.   If she continues to apply herself, Helen will undoubtedly have a bright and promising future.

Our Assessment: Where do I start?   I have no idea what relationship the author has with the candidate, because she fails to reveal it.   As a result, I have no way of putting her comments into perspective.   Second, she fails to provide any new information about Helen, other than that she used to be immature and uncommitted.   Although the author seems impressed by Helen's entrepreneurial skills, she did not highlight them in any meaningful way.   Even worse, she qualifies her actual recommendation in the final paragraph with a huge "if."   By failing to provide any details about Helen's amazing transformation, the author missed a golden opportunity to sell her to a highly competitive business program.

Letter #43: Ambivalent Letter

Melanie Riggs is a bright and energetic young woman who has assumed numerous leadership positions at Antioch College.   As her advisor in the Biochemistry Department, I have been her professor in three classes, in which Melanie received "B" grades.

Compared to her peers in the department, Melanie is an above- average student.   At times, she gives 100% to her studies and amazes us with her performance; other times, Melanie becomes overwhelmed and does not live up to her true potential.   From my perspective, this may be due to maturity issues; in every respect, Melanie seems to be a late bloomer.

Despite her motivational issues, Melanie has managed to accelerate academically, taking senior level classes during her junior year. This fall, Melanie has enrolled in a graduate level course in Biochemistry, which requires substantial lab time and a significant amount of outside preparation. Thankfully, Melanie has been able to handle this new challenge in addition to her other academic commitments.

Melanie's impressive participation in the Business Club confirms her potential for success as a leader.   We believe that she is "stepping up to the plate" for the next chapter in her life, and once established in business school, she will be able to reveal the gifts that we know she possesses.   We are happy to recommend her to your institution.

Our Assessment: Although filled with compliments, this letter sabotaged Melanie's chance to get into business school.   The second paragraph, which describes her as "a late bloomer" and "not living up to her true potential," told the committee that Melanie was NOT a serious student.   Even worse is the author's frequent use of the term "we," which implies that she is speaking not just for herself, but for her entire department.   Business school is a serious endeavor; it should not be the first time that a candidate "steps to the plate" and fulfills his/her potential.   Sadly, this type of ambivalence in an academic reference letter will tank even the strongest application.

Letter #44:   Nothing but the Facts

Samantha Jones worked for me as an Assistant Accountant at the Hilton Hotel from December of 2003 to August of 2005.   During that time, she was promoted once and received two annual raises.   Her performance reviews were "Above Average," noting her efficiency and organizational skills.   All of her assignments, including our annual tax return, were completed on time and within expectations.

Samantha left the Hilton Hotel to accept a position as a Junior Accountant at the Ramada Inn in Cambridge.   We were sorry to see her go.   We wish Samantha all the best in the future.

Our Assessment: This letters includes positive information, but not nearly enough to make an admissions decision. By failing to discuss Samantha's strengths, or relate them to the requirements of business school, the author gave the reader no reason to be enthusiastic about her.   In fact, by providing such a terse letter, the author made the committee wonder what she WASN'T saying.

Letter #45:   Mild Sabotage

It is a pleasure to recommend Michael Hightower to Wharton School of Business.   An active young man with a love of the outdoors, Michael has a highly adventurous spirit.   Consequently, he is excited about the prospect of enrolling in your school's unique curriculum in Environmental Law.

Michael has attended Barrington College since his sophomore year.   Over the past three years, he has developed a strong personality and a deep sense of purpose.   As a high school senior, Michael was diagnosed with a learning disability that required a customized approach to studying.   He transferred to Barrington College after his freshman year, when the large state university he attended did not provide the level of support that he desired.   Michael has done much better on our small, close-knit campus.   Although he was often frustrated, he worked hard to master subject areas that were incredibly difficult for him.   Thanks to the tireless support of his advisor, Dr. Wong, Michael was able to find his place on campus.

By completing college one semester early, Michael has cleared his schedule to participate in a one-semester program at the University of Alaska, where he will research the dioxin levels in swordfish.   The data he is gathering will be used to support a university research project on environmental safety in rural food supplies.   The skills that Michael is developing in data collection and management will be well-utilized in his graduate studies.

I applaud Michael's willingness to participate in such a challenging venture, considering his previous problems adjusting to new situations.   Thankfully, the program in Alaska is well-organized and well-supervised.   By the time Michael gets to Wharton, he will already have several critical skills under his belt, including the ability to thrive in a large, unknown environment.

By pursuing the program in Alaska, Michael has shown us that he knows how to set a goal and see it through. His initiative has set a precedent for our school and has inspired his fellow students to set similarly high expectations. Accordingly, Michael has the potential to be a role model for others by channeling his energy into the work he loves best.   I wish Michael the best in his pursuit of a business education.

Our Assessment: This letter appears to have been written by two different people: one who supports Michael, and another who thinks he is immature and incapable of handling adult responsibilities.   By mentioning his problems adapting to life situations, the author negated all of the great things he said about Michael's work in Alaska.   He repeatedly called attention to a negative, rather than cite the candidate's strengths.   As a result, the reader walks away confused about how strongly the author is endorsing Michael.

Summary

After reading this book, including 45 actual reference letters, we hope that you feel well-prepared to write (or obtain) a persuasive letter of recommendation for business school.

A Quick Summary for Candidates:

1. Ask people who know you well enough to highlight your strengths (and are willing to do so).

2. Give each author enough information to do a good job for you, including:

   a. a cover letter with the names, addresses and deadlines for all of the letters you need   (Appendix 2)
   b. the appropriate forms from each school that the writer needs to complete
   c. a summary of your "Match Points" (Appendix 3)
   d. a current copy of your resume
   e. your personal statement
   f. pre-addressed, stamped envelopes for all letters

3. Give the author enough time to write a compelling letter.

4. Follow through with each author to ensure that his/her letter reaches its destination.

5. Thank the author for his/her efforts on your behalf.

A Quick Summary for Letter Writers:

1. Meet with the candidate to determine whether you are the best person to write a reference letter on his/her behalf.

2. If you agree to write a letter, give the candidate a copy of the Reference Letter Request Form (Appendix 5), which summarizes all of the information you will need.

3. Do not begin until you have all of the requested documents.

4. Before putting pen to paper, be sure to review your organization's policy regarding letters of recommendation. Limit your comments to positive, factual observations that you have actually observed in your interactions with the applicant.

5. Follow our guidelines in Chapter 5 to write the best letter possible.

6. For additional help in writing and editing letters of recommendation, admissions essays, and personal statements, please visit www.ivyleagueadmission.com.

In the MBA application process, reference letters can provide the committee with objective, third-party documentation of a candidate's strengths and skills.   A well-crafted reference letter can also explain a variety of personal circumstances (and obstacles) better than any personal statement ever could.   By harnessing the power of your recommendations, you will improve your chances of gaining admission to the top business schools in the country. Don't miss this chance to claim your destiny!

Appendices

Appendix 1:   Sample Rating Sheet

Appendix 2:   Request for Reference Letters

Appendix 3:   Sample Match Points

Appendix 4:   Sample Thank You Note for a Reference Letter

Appendix 5:   Reference Letter Request Form

Appendix 1:   Sample Rating Sheet

Factors: For each factor below, please indicate your opinion of this applicant's rating on that factor relative to other candidates you have observed.

Ranking Standards:

1. Exceptional, top 5%
2. Excellent, next 10%
3. Good, next 20%

4. Average, middle 30%
5. Reservation, next 30%
6. Poor, low 5%

7. No basis for judgment

Factors:

_____   **Emotional Stability:**   Exhibits stable moods; performs under pressure

_____   **Interpersonal Relations:**   Rapport with others; cooperation, attitude toward supervisors

_____   **Judgment:**   Ability to analyze problems, common sense; decisiveness

_____   **Resourcefulness:**   Originality; initiative, management of resources and time

_____   **Reliability:**   Dependability; sense of responsibility, promptness; conscientiousness

_____   **Perseverance:**   Stamina; endurance, psychological strength

_____   **Communication skills:**   Clarity in writing and speech

_____   **Self-confidence:** Assuredness; awareness of strengths & weaknesses

_____   **Empathy:**   Consideration; tact; sensitivity to the needs of others

_____   **Maturity:**   Personal development; social awareness, ability to cope with life situations

_____   **Intellectual curiosity:**   Desire to learn and extend beyond expectations

_____   **Scholarship:** Ability to learn, quality of study habits, native intellectual ability

_____   **Motivation:**   Depth of commitment; intensity; sincerity of career choice

Evaluation Summary:

Compared to other business school applicants you know, please provide an overall evaluation of this candidate:

(   ) Exceptional candidate, top 5%
(   ) Excellent candidate, next 10%
(   ) Good candidate, next 20%

(   ) Average candidate, middle 30%
(   ) Weak candidate, bottom 35%
(   ) No basis for judgment

Appendix 2:   Request for Reference Letters

Name: Date:

Address: Phone: Email:

Dr./Mr./Mrs./Ms.   _____,

I appreciate your willingness to write me a strong letter of recommendation for business school.   This page summarizes the schools to which I am applying and the name(s) and address(es) of each person to whom the letter(s) should be addressed.   For your convenience, I have listed the schools in the order in which the letters need to be received (the earliest deadlines are listed first).

I am enclosing several pages of supporting information:

a)   A list of my Match Points, which explain how my credentials match the school's requirements
c)   A current copy of my resume
d)   My personal statement
e)   Pre-addressed, stamped envelopes for all letters

Please let me know if you need additional information.   Thank you for your support.

1)   School 1:   Name and Address of School
                  Name of Contact Person to Whom Letter Should be Addressed
                  Date Letter Should be Mailed to School
                  Additional Information / Instructions (if any)

2)   School 2:   Name and Address of School
                  Name of Contact Person to Whom Letter Should be Addressed
                  Date Letter Should be Mailed to School
                  Additional Information / Instructions (if any)

3)   School 3:   Name and Address of School
                  Name of Contact Person to Whom Letter Should be Addressed
                  Date Letter Should be Mailed to School
                  Additional Information / Instructions (if any)

If you have any questions or concerns, please contact me at the phone number and email address above.   Thank you again for your support.

Appendix 3:   Bethany Daniel's Preparation for Business School (Match Points)

My Preparation:

1)   **Academic Preparation**.   My academic and professional background are an excellent match for business school. I hold a BA in Chemistry from Brown University and an MS in Public Health from Harvard University.   I earned a GPA of 4.0 in both programs, despite working a full-time job at the same time.

2)   **Professional Experience**.   I have also cultivated extensive interpersonal experience in both educational and public health environments to verify my suitability for a business career.

As a teacher, I learned to communicate scientific concepts to non-scientists.   I developed my public speaking skills and promoted myself as a scientific leader throughout the state.   I enjoyed being a role model for students and getting them excited about chemistry.   I valued the trust they placed in me and the long-term friendships I have made in the process.

As a public health manager, I implemented an AIDS awareness program in my community.   I also develop educational booklets about disease prevention and give lectures to interested groups in the county.   I supervise a group of lab technicians and am responsible for the actual testing and reporting of results.   I thrive in my role as a counselor, particularly to young women and children.   I am eager to pursue a career as a public health advocate.

3)   **Outside Interests**.   I am a tri-athlete who competes at the state, local and national levels.   I also am a volunteer paramedic for the local ambulance company.

4)   **Sincerity of Interest**.   My interest in business school is a natural progression of my career in public health. Through my work, I have identified the need for increased funding and more effective programs to serve inner city patients who are at an increased risk for HIV, hepatitis and other sexually transmitted diseases.   With an MBA, I will have the knowledge and skills to fill that need.

With my excellent academic background, strong interpersonal skills, and commitment to helping others, I am a great fit for this career.   I am certain that I have the diligence, stamina, and emotional stability that are needed to complete a business degree.   At age 30, I also possess the maturity to pursue my education with purpose and enthusiasm.

How My Credentials Match the School's Requirements:

As my major professor in graduate school, you supervised all aspects of my class work and clinical training.   These are the experiences and strengths that I hope you will mention in your reference letter:

a.   Intellectual Drive: completed 45 graduate hours in public health, including two courses (PH 477 and PH 555) that are normally restricted to doctoral candidates.   Attained a perfect 4.0 GPA.

b.   Research Skills: completed an independent research project on HIV transmission in Ghana;   results were published in *JAMA*.

c.   Teaching Skills: during my year in Ghana, I helped to establish a pre-school in an underserved area.   During the summer of 2004, I returned to the region under the auspices of Doctors Without Borders, which helped me to expand the original curriculum.

d.   Communication Skills: excellent speaker and writer; I have published 5 articles in peer-reviewed journals and presented 3 papers at national public health seminars at Harvard.   During the summer of 2005, I hosted my own talk show, Healthier Lives, on public access television (Channel 1).

e.   Empathy & Motivation: I work well with people from diverse racial and socioeconomic backgrounds.   I have also assumed leadership responsibilities beyond the scope of my job, with a continual eye on developing my skills as a public health advocate.

Appendix 4:   Sample Thank You Note for a Reference Letter

October 1, 2009

Lawrence Johnson, Esq.
Johnson & Taylor Legal Services
333 Island Drive
Warren, CT   02876

Dear Mr. Johnson,

Thank you for taking the time to write a recommendation letter to support my business school application.   I appreciate the timeliness of your reply and the gracious compliments in your letter.

My motivation to obtain my MBA stems from the two satisfying summers that I worked at your firm.   My first-hand experience with you and your staff was instrumental in my decision to pursue a career in executive sales.   Thank you for giving me the opportunity to work with such high profile accounts at a pivotal point in my career.

I will contact you during the admissions process to apprise you of my progress.   Thank you again for the reference letter and for your kindness to me over the years.   You've been an exceptional mentor and role model.

Sincerely,

Erica Page

Appendix 5:   Reference Letter Request Form

Thank you for inquiring about the possibility of obtaining a reference letter from me.   Please follow these steps to ensure that I can do a great job on your behalf.

Step 1:   Arrange an Initial Meeting to Discuss the Letter

Please schedule a meeting with me to talk about the recommendation letter **at least four weeks before** you need it. Ask me if I would feel comfortable writing a supportive and positive recommendation for you.

When asked to provide a reference, I have to ask myself if I know you well enough to support your application for a particular graduate program. Acknowledging the importance of a top-quality endorsement, I would rather decline the request to write a reference than write a vague or mediocre one.   Let's meet face-to-face to discuss whether or not I am the right person to write your letter.

Step 2: Provide All Relevant Documentation

If we agree that I should write your letter during our face-to-face meeting, please be prepared to provide the following documents:

    a.   A cover sheet with the names, addresses and deadlines for all of the letters you need
    b.   The appropriate forms from each school that I will need to complete
    c.   A ONE-page summary of the accomplishments you want me to mention
    d.   A current copy of your resume (including your awards, publications and honors)
    e.   Your personal statement
    f.   Pre-addressed, stamped envelopes for all letters

Also feel free to include ONE page of additional information that you feel will help me write the letter.   This may include specific anecdotes and stories you want me to mention, along with additional details about projects or papers I have seen that would demonstrate your creativity, intelligence, writing abilities or technical skills.

Please type all information. You should waive your right to read the letter of recommendation, keeping in mind that I will still give you a copy for your records.

Note: I will NOT write the letter unless I have all of the documents listed above.

Step 3: Follow-up

Once I receive the documents, I will confirm an exact date that your letter will be sent.   One week after the expected date of arrival, please verify that the letter has reached its destination.   If the business school has NOT received the letter within 10 days, please let me know.   I will send another copy.

Thank you for adhering to these guidelines.

Professor John Smith, 111 Rogers Hall, (555)-555-5555, jsmith@college.edu